Superworld
Activity Book 1

Name ....

Class ....

Look!

Extra activities   page 40

My picture dictionary   page 57

Cut outs   page 67

Carol Read   Ana Soberón

MACMILLAN

The dragon eggs

1 **Match and colour**

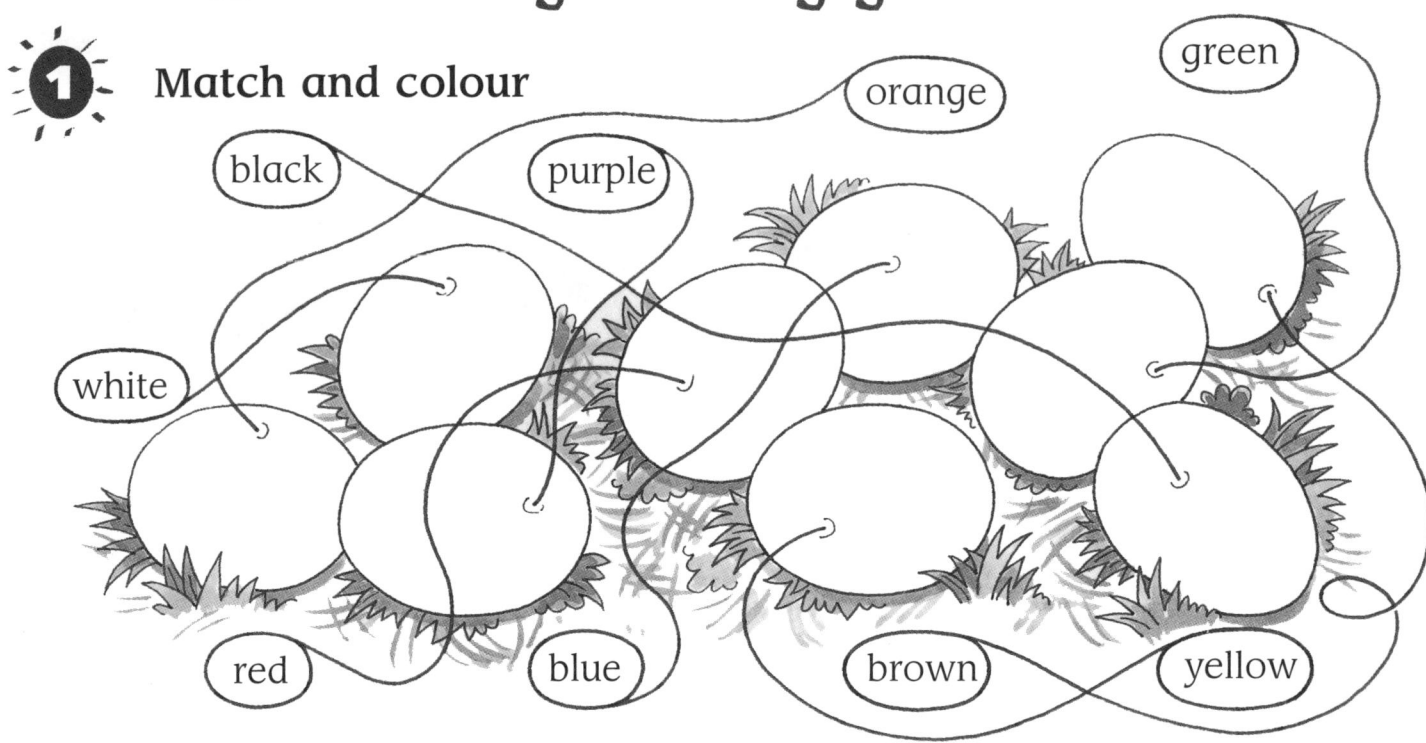

green

orange

black   purple

white

red   blue   brown   yellow

2 **Find the colour words**

Write a list.

.... red ....

....

....

....

....

....

....

....

....

a l b l a c k a b
w h i t e f h s y
b o i w l b l u e
r r y p h e m g l
o a o l y i o r l
w n s w d h t e o
n g t r e d r e w
r e o c w l p n i
i e s p u r p l e

3  Listen, colour and write

| tree | ~~fish~~ | flower | bird |

1 The ......*fish*...... is orange.

2 The .... is yellow.

3 The .... is green.

4 The .... is red.

1

4 **Mix the colours**

Write the answers.

1   Mix (yellow) and (blue.

   What colour is the fish?

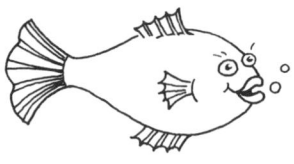

.......*green*...........

2   Mix (red,) (blue) and (yellow.

   What colour is the tree?

....

3   Mix (yellow) and (red.

   What colour is the bird?

....

4   Mix (blue) and (red.

   What colour is the flower?

....

5 **Do a group survey**

What's your favourite colour?

Red.

Name	Favourite colour

6 **Colour and write**

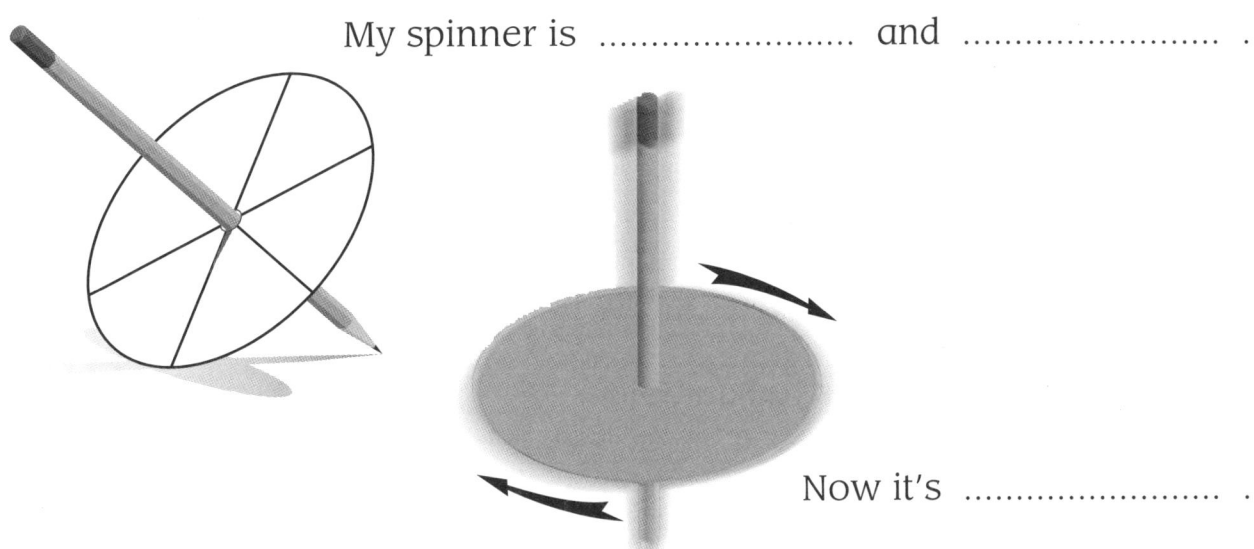

My spinner is .... and ....

Now it's ....

7 **Play colour bingo**

BINGO!

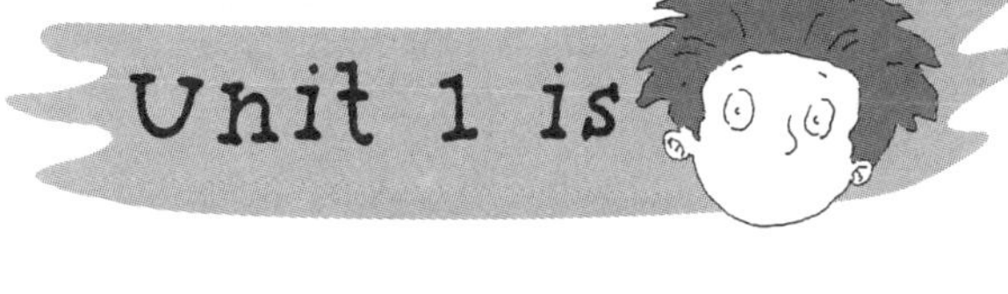

Unit 1 is

Beetles and butterflies

1 **Read and colour**

1 The grasshopper is green.

2 The butterfly is purple.

3 The snail is brown and white.

4 The spider is brown.

5 The ladybird is red and black.

2 **Look and write**

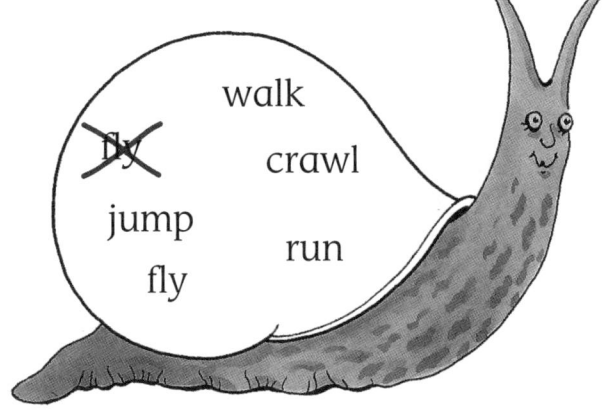

walk

~~fly~~

crawl

jump

run

fly

1 Butterflies ....*fly*.... .

2 Snails ....

3 Grasshoppers ....

4 Beetles ....

5 Spiders ....

6 Ladybirds ....

3 **Complete the chart**

Are you scared of ...?   Tick (✔)

ME	Yes						
	No						
MY FRIEND	Yes						
	No						

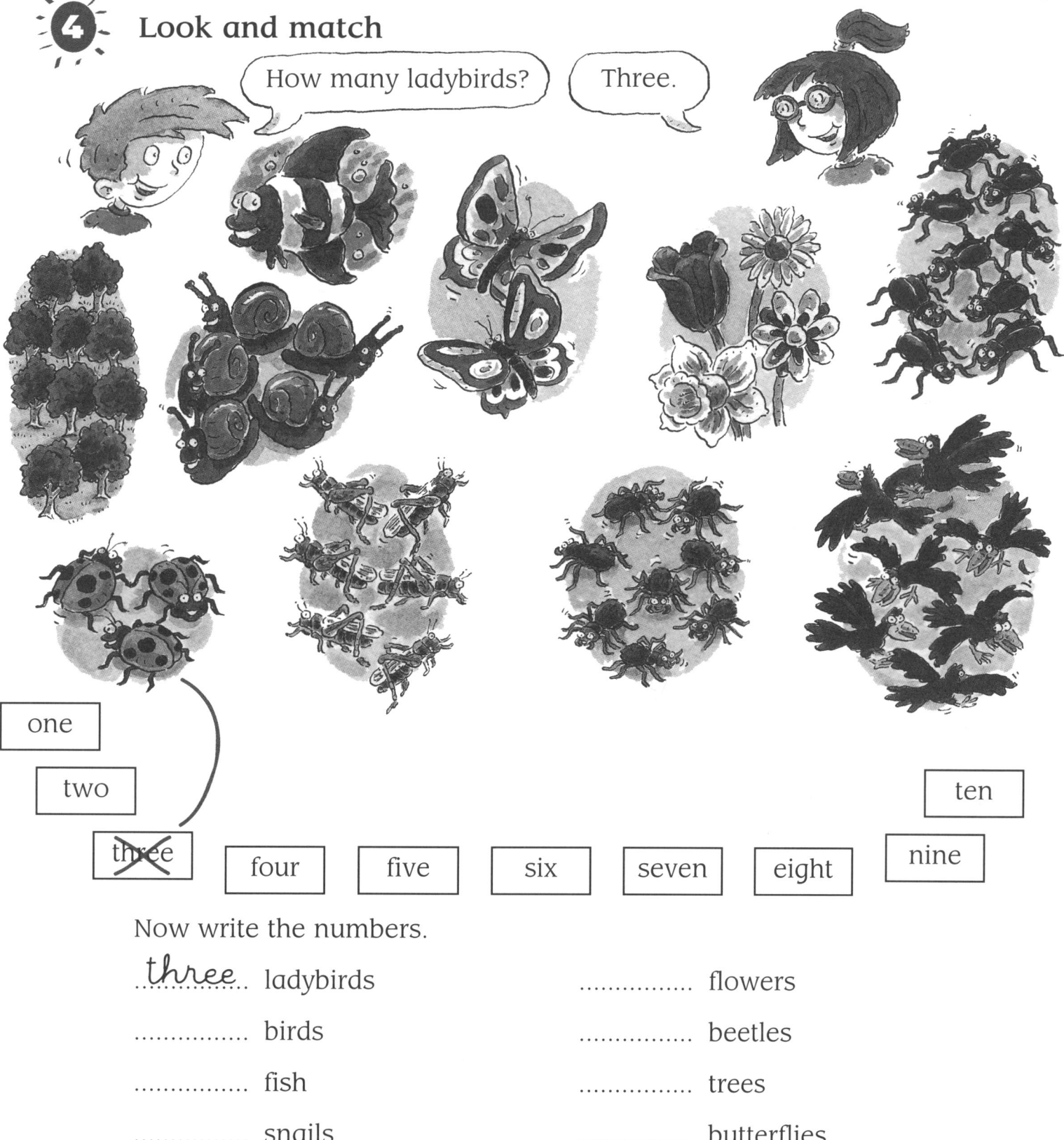

4 Look and match

How many ladybirds? Three.

one

two

~~three~~

four   five   six   seven   eight

nine

ten

Now write the numbers.

three ladybirds   .... flowers

.... birds   .... beetles

.... fish   .... trees

.... snails   .... butterflies

.... grasshoppers   .... spiders

5 **Read, count and colour**

The animal with no legs is blue.

The animals with six legs are red.

The animal with eight legs is green.

6 **Classify the animals**

| ~~butterflies~~ ladybirds snails beetles spiders grasshoppers |

Animals with six legs
butterflies,

Animals with eight legs

Animals with no legs

7 Find a partner

What's your name?

How old are you?

I'm .....Marta Spider..... .
I'm .....eight..... years old.

I'm ....
I'm .... years old.

8 Look and count

1 How many spiders? .....eight..................... .

2 How many ladybirds? ....

3 How many grasshoppers? ....

4 How many butterflies? ....

5 How many beetles? ....

6 How many snails? ....

Unit 2 is

1 Look and match

rainbow

witch

butterfly

frog

parrot

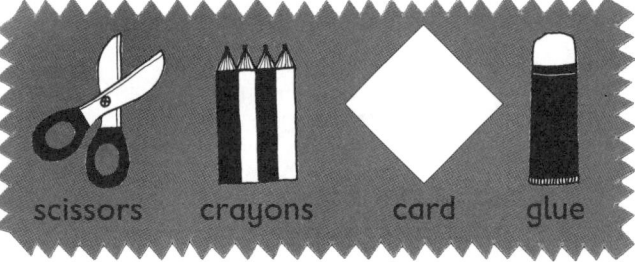

2 Make story cards (page 73)

scissors   crayons   card   glue

3 Listen to the story

This is the story of Rod the frog.

Hold up the cards.

4 Act out the story

5 Complete the dialogue

| witch | Goodbye | Green | ~~Hello~~ |

..........Hello.......... , Rod. Why are you sad?

.... is horrible.
I want to be like you.

Go and see the .... at the
end of the rainbow.

That's a good idea.
....

6 Write and colour

I'm the butterfly. I'm ....yellow...... ,
.... and ....

I'm the parrot. I'm .... ,
.... and ....

Fun in class

1 Label the pictures

rubber

pencil

~~pen~~

ruler

pencil case

book

pencil sharpener

1 ....pen........

2 ....

3 ....

4 ....

5 ....

6 ....

7 ....

2 Write answers

1 What's this?   It's a ....rubber.... .

2 What's this?   It's a ....

3 What's this?   It's a ....

3 Look and match

20

11

17

14

18

eleven
twelve
thirteen
fourteen
fifteen
sixteen
seventeen
eighteen
nineteen
twenty

15

12

19

16

13

4 Count and write

....*fourteen*.... pencils

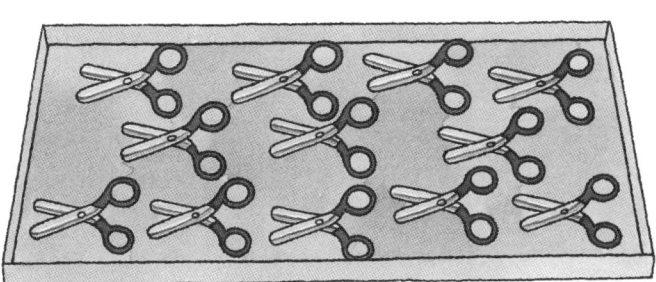

.... scissors

.... pencil sharpeners

.... rubbers

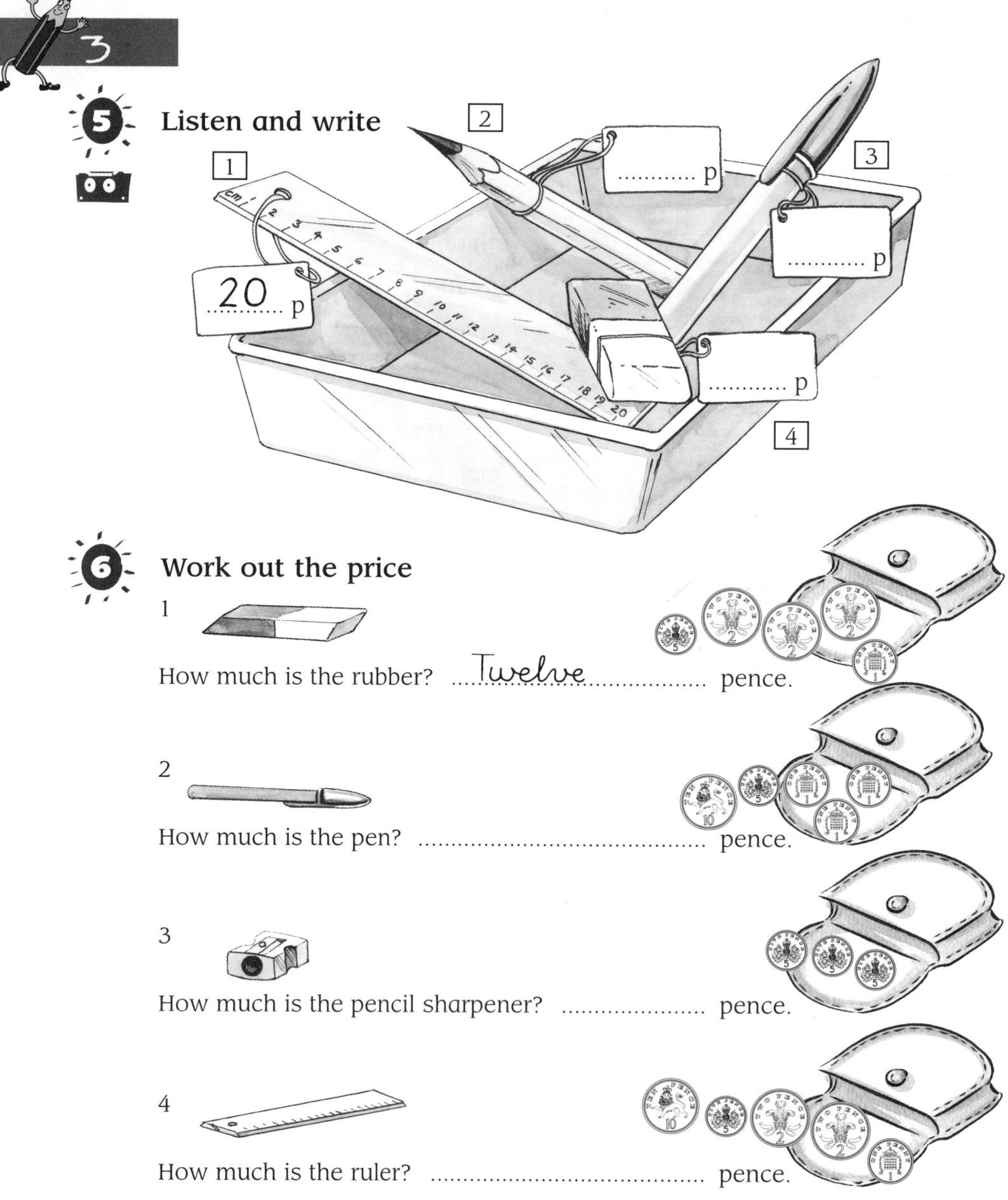

3

5 Listen and write

1

2 .... p

3 .... p

20 p

4 .... p

6 Work out the price

1

How much is the rubber? ....Twelve.................. pence.

2

How much is the pen? .... pence.

3

How much is the pencil sharpener? .... pence.

4

How much is the ruler? .... pence.

7 Make a shopping list

Things to buy	Price
....	....
....	....
....	....
....	....

8 Complete the dialogue

| Thank you | Goodbye | 10p | ~~Hello~~ |

Hello.

..........Hello.................. .

How much is the rubber, please?

....

Here you are.

....

Goodbye.

....

Unit 3 is

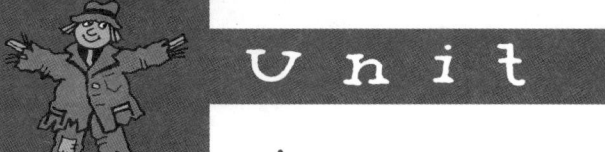

Scarecrows and skeletons

1 Read and colour the scarecrow

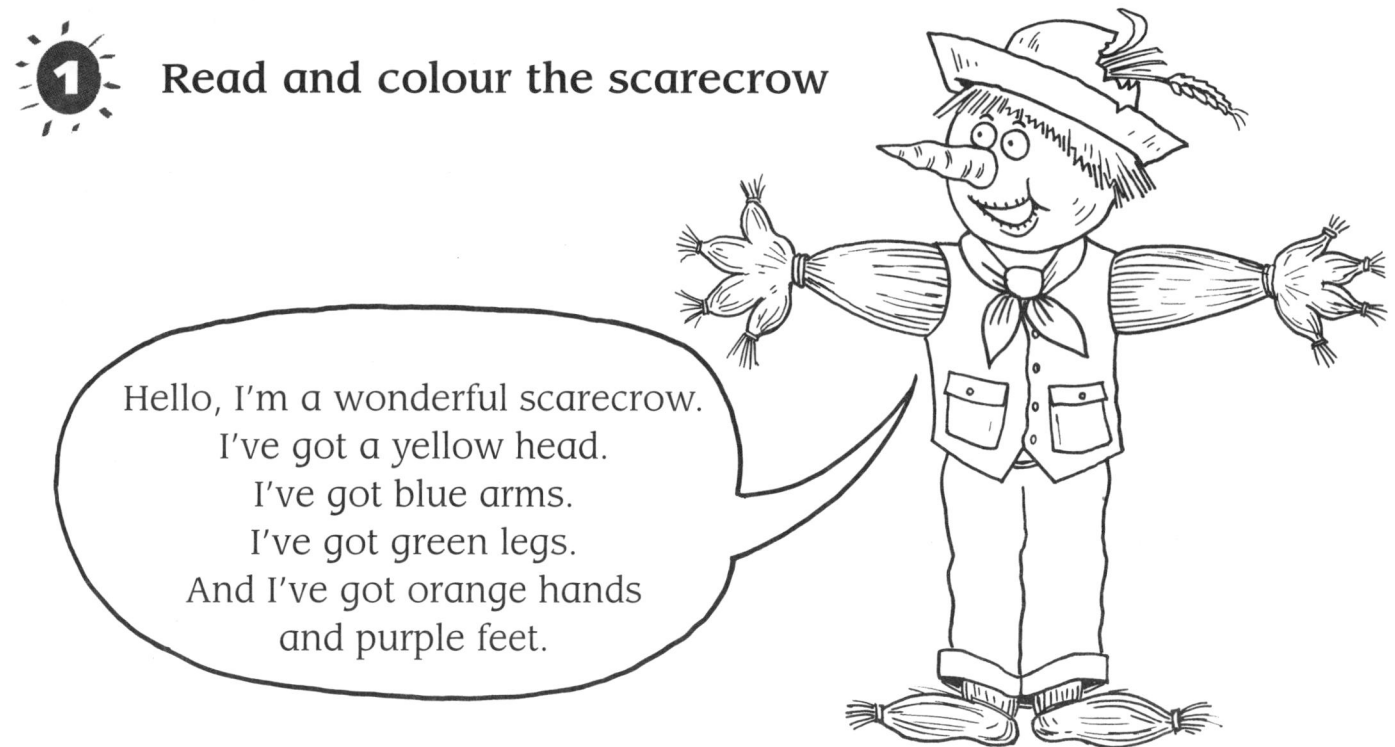

Hello, I'm a wonderful scarecrow.
I've got a yellow head.
I've got blue arms.
I've got green legs.
And I've got orange hands
and purple feet.

2 Look and label

| hands | ~~legs~~ | arms | head | feet |

legs

3 Listen and number

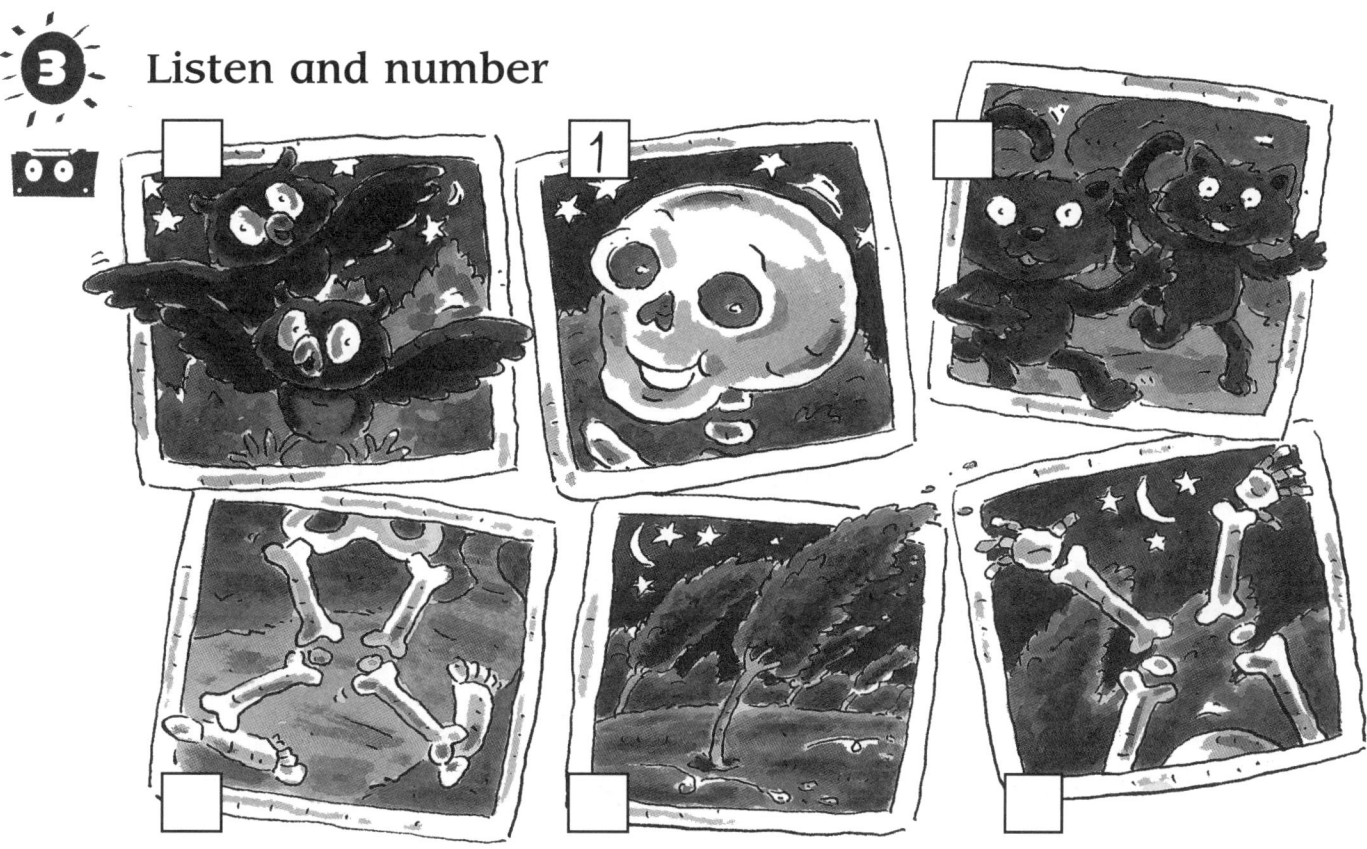

4 Write a scary story

One dark night, ... goes for a walk.

His  ...._feet_.............. go .... !

His .... go .... !

His .... go .... !

Bang, bang, bang! The door opens. Creak, creak, creak!

Hello, ... Welcome to the party!

5 Write *big* or *small*

I've got ....**big**...... feet.

I've got a ....**small**.. nose.

I've got .... ears.

I've got .... eyes.

I've got .... hands.

I've got a .... mouth.

6 Read and draw

Tanya is Molly's friend. She's got big eyes and small ears. She's got a small nose and a small mouth. She's got brown hair.

Sam is Ted's friend. He's got small eyes and big ears. He's got a small nose and a small mouth. He's got black hair.

 **7** **Describe two friends**

..........Maria.......... is my friend. She's got .....big eyes and black hair....

.... is my friend. She's got ....

.... is my friend. He's got ....

Now play a guessing game.

 **8** **Look and complete**

| mouth | ~~eyes~~ | nose | ears | ears | eyes | mouth | nose |

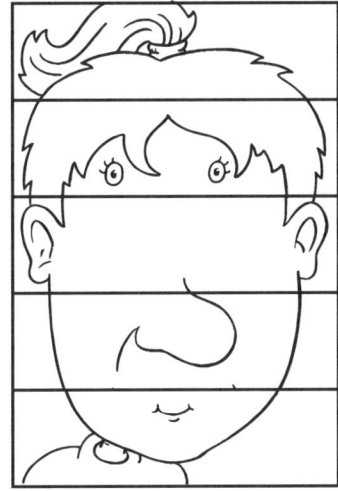

1 He's got big ....eyes......

and small ....

He's got a small ....

and a big ....

2 She's got small ....

and big ....

She's got a big ....

and a small ....

Unit 4 is

Unit 5

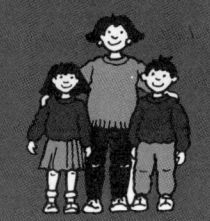

A family for Danny

1 Write the family words

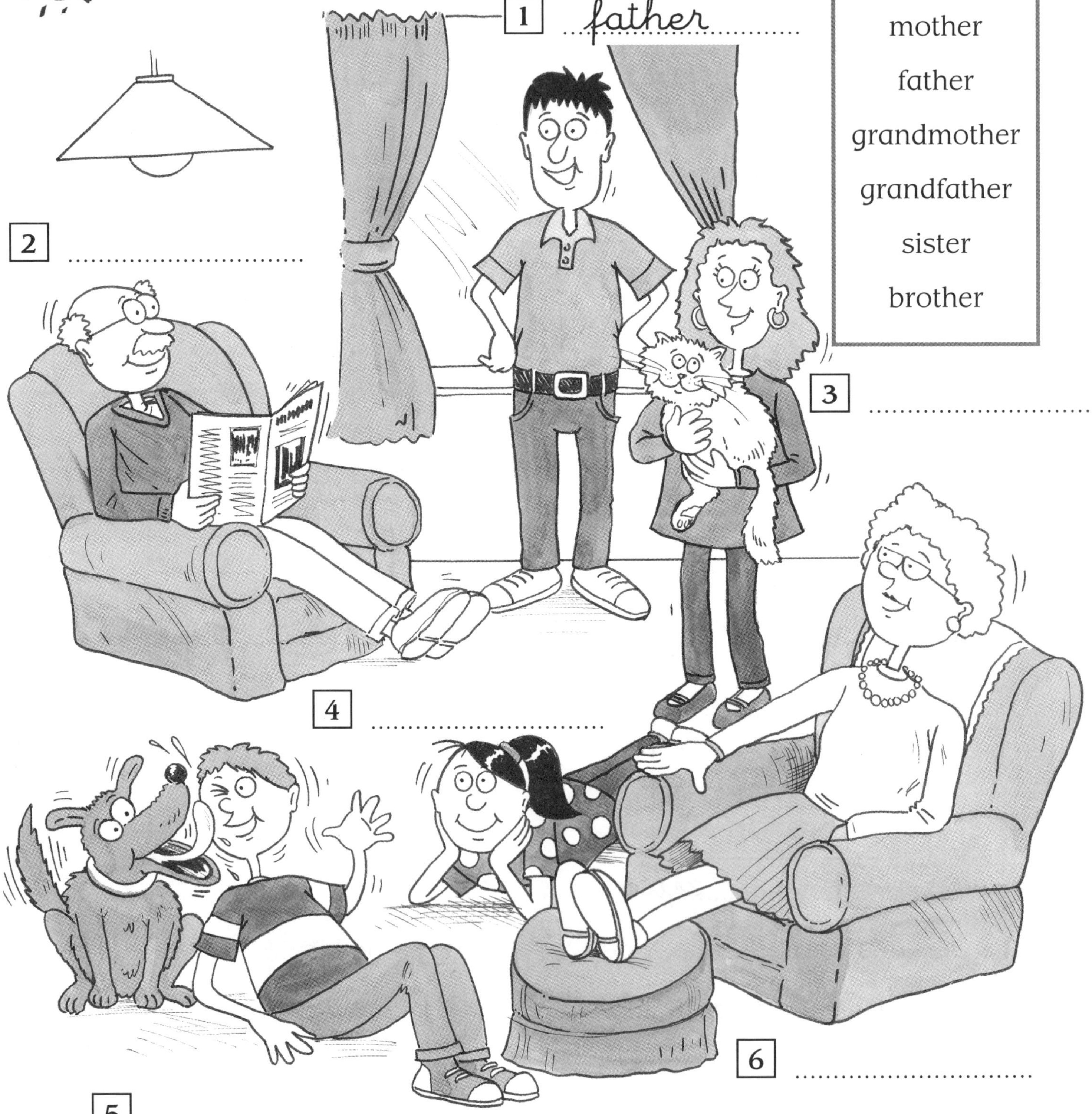

1 father
2 ....
3 ....
4 ....
5 ....
6 ....

mother
father
grandmother
grandfather
sister
brother

2 Read and circle the answers

1	Danny has got a mother.	Yes	(No)
2	Danny has got a father.	Yes	No
3	Danny has got a grandmother.	Yes	No
4	Danny has got a grandfather.	Yes	No
5	Danny has got brothers and sisters.	Yes	No
6	Danny has got two friends.	Yes	No

3 Do a group survey

Write *yes* or *no*

Have you got a ...	ME			
brother?				
sister?				
cat?				
dog?				

5

4 Listen, colour and complete

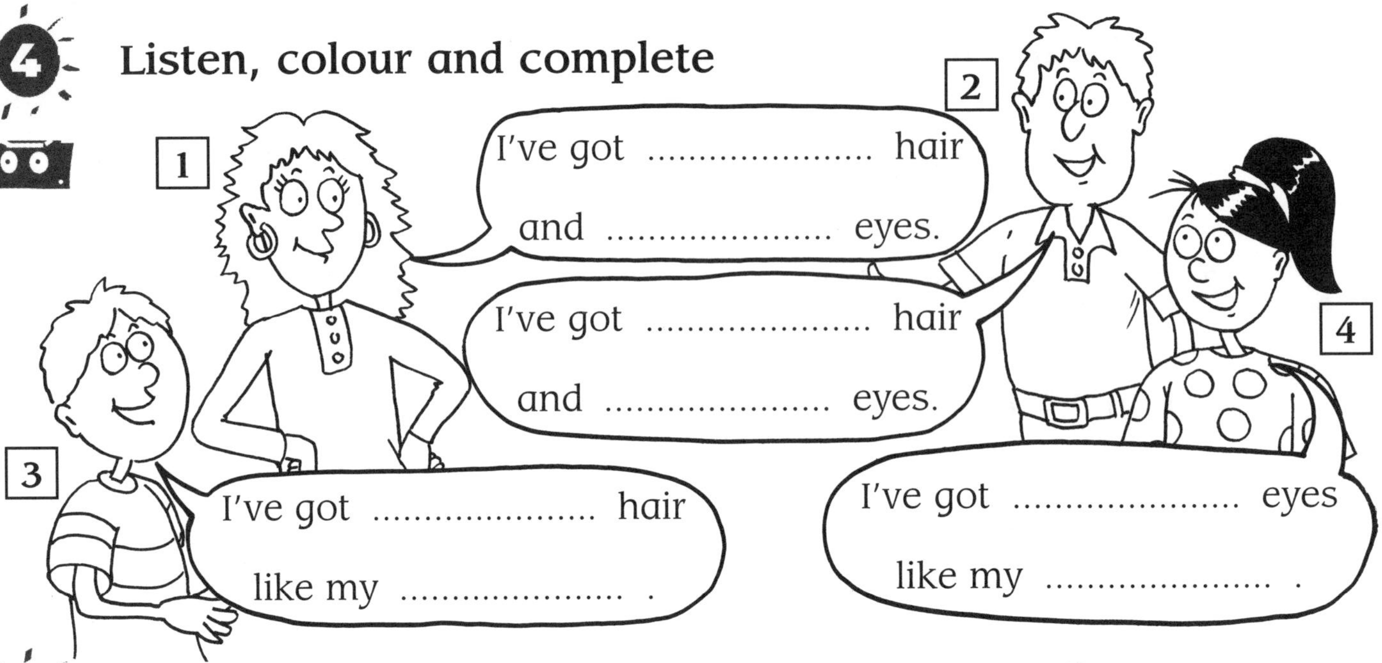

1

I've got .... hair

and .... eyes.

2

I've got .... hair

and .... eyes.

3

I've got .... hair

like my ....

4

I've got .... eyes

like my ....

5 Colour the hair and eyes for your family

My mother

My father

My brother

My sister

Me

Now complete the sentences.

I've got ....*brown*.......... *hair*.. like my ....*mother*..... .

My sister has got ....*blue*....... *eyes*... like my ....*father*...... .

1 I've got .... like my ....

2 My sister has got .... like my ....

3 My brother has got .... like my ....

6   Read and identify the picture

This is a picture of my family.

I've got black hair like my mother.

My grandfather has got black hair too.

My brother has got fair hair.

My cat has got small ears and big eyes!

7   Draw and write about your family

This is a picture of my family.

I've got ....

My .... has got

....

My .... has got

....

My .... has got

....

Unit 5 is

Food, delicious food!

1 Look and match

banana   carrot   ham   apple

tomato   lettuce   pizza   egg

sandwich   chicken   hamburger   cheese

2 Look and write   I like or I don't like

...........I like........... ice cream.

.... cheese.

.... bananas.

3 Do a group survey

Do you like ...?   (✓) = Yes, I do.   (✗) = No, I don't.

	Me			
eggs	✗			

 **Answer the questions**

 Yes, I do.  No, I don't.

1   Do you like carrots? ....

2   Do you like hamburgers? ....

3   Do you like lettuce? ....

4   Do you like chicken? ....

5   Do you like apples? ....

Now write two questions to ask a friend.

.... ?

.... ?

5 **Write about your sandwich**

In my sandwich I've got

.... , ...

and ....

I like ....

sandwiches.

I don't like ....

sandwiches.

Stick your sandwich here.

6 Look and count

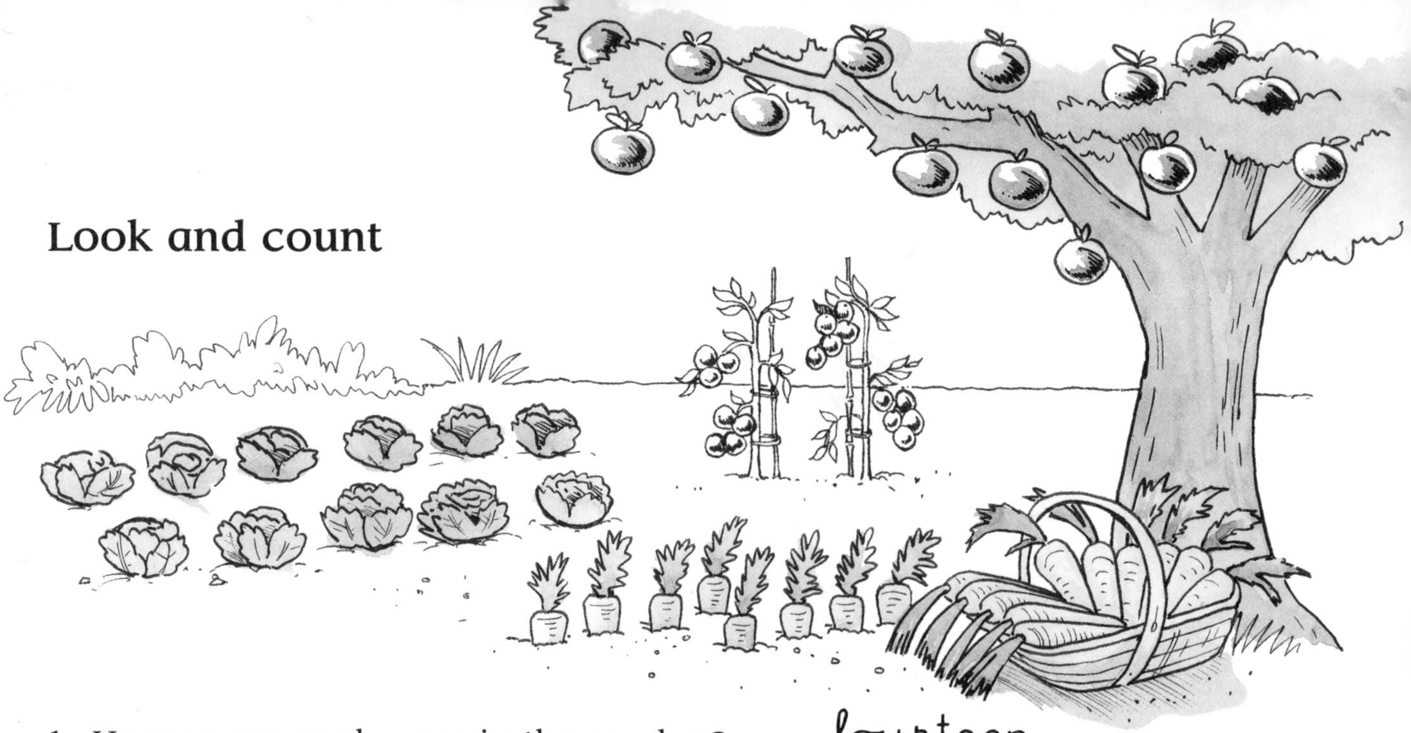

1 How many apples are in the garden? ...... *fourteen* ....

2 How many lettuces are in the garden? ....

3 How many tomatoes are in the garden? ....

4 How many carrots are in the garden? ....

7 Classify the food

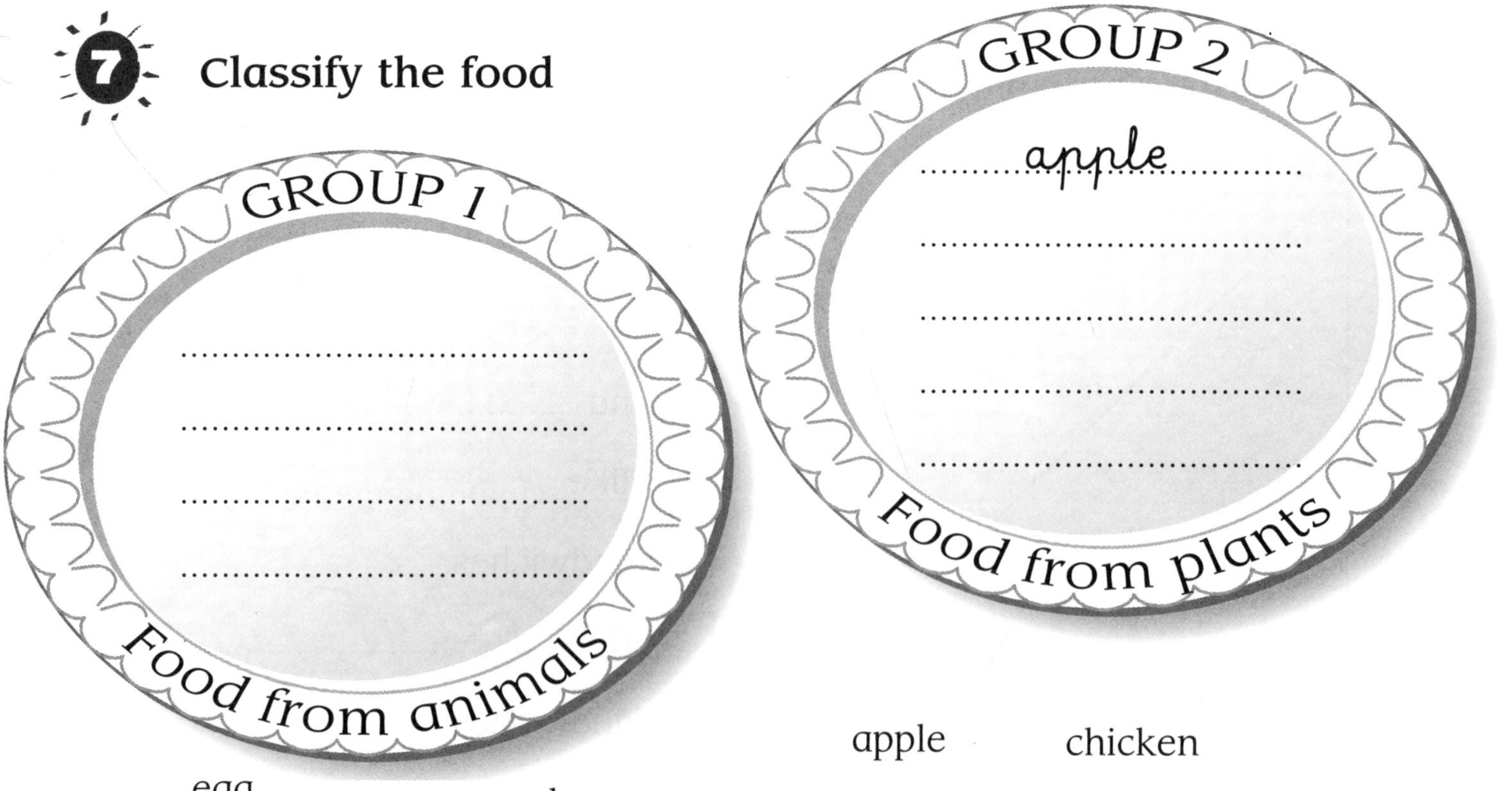

GROUP 1

....
....
....
....

Food from animals

GROUP 2

...... *apple* ....
....
....
....
....

Food from plants

apple   chicken

egg   banana   ham

lettuce   carrot   cheese   tomato

 **Do a flower experiment**

white flower

glass of red water

Put the flower in a glass of red water.

Guess what happens. Tick (✔)

The flower goes red in ...

one day. ☐

two days. ☐

three days. ☐

four days. ☐

Draw a picture and write the result.

The flower goes red in

.... days.

1 **Make the story characters** (page 85)

scissors crayons glue

2 **Listen to the story**

Move the characters.

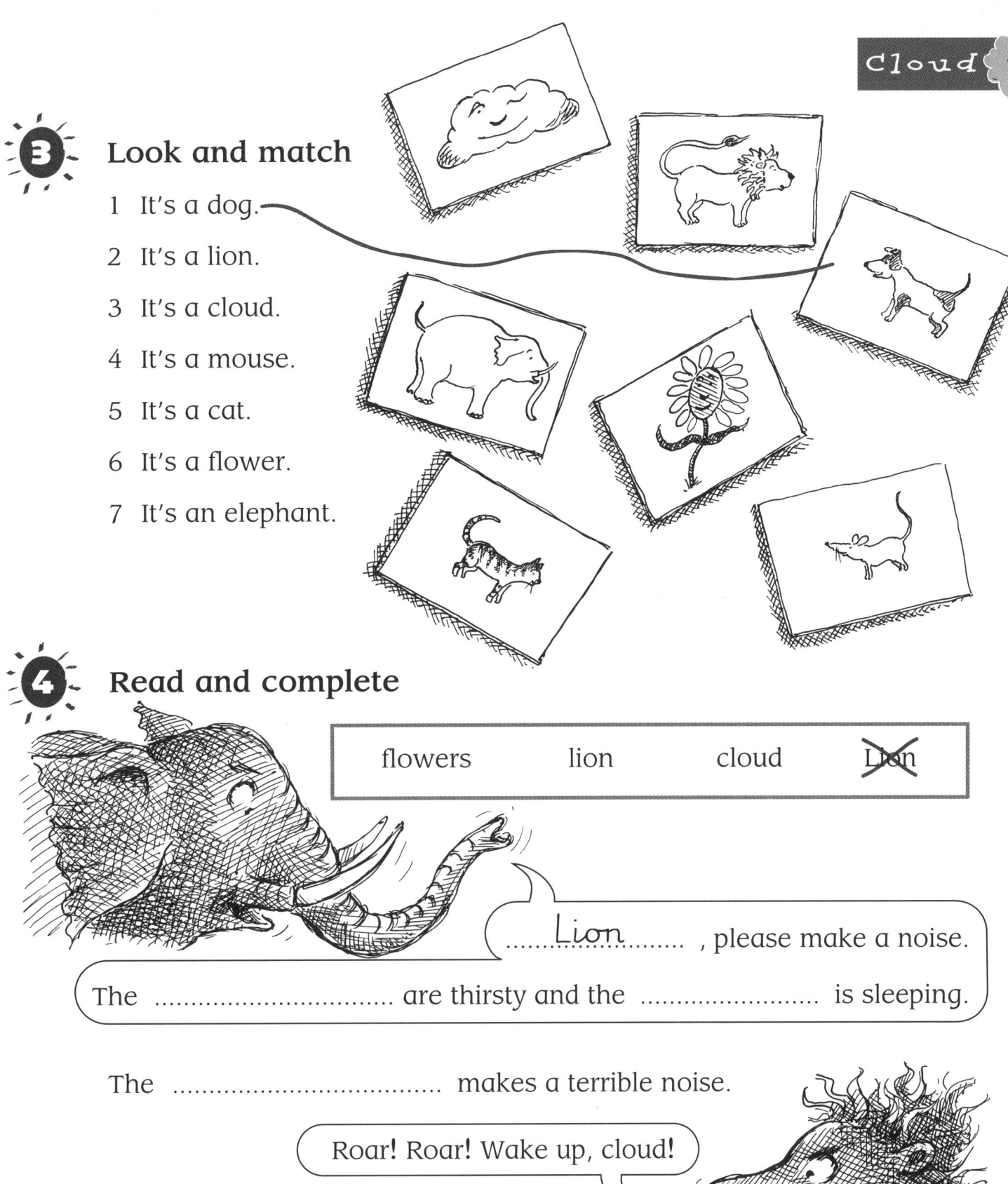

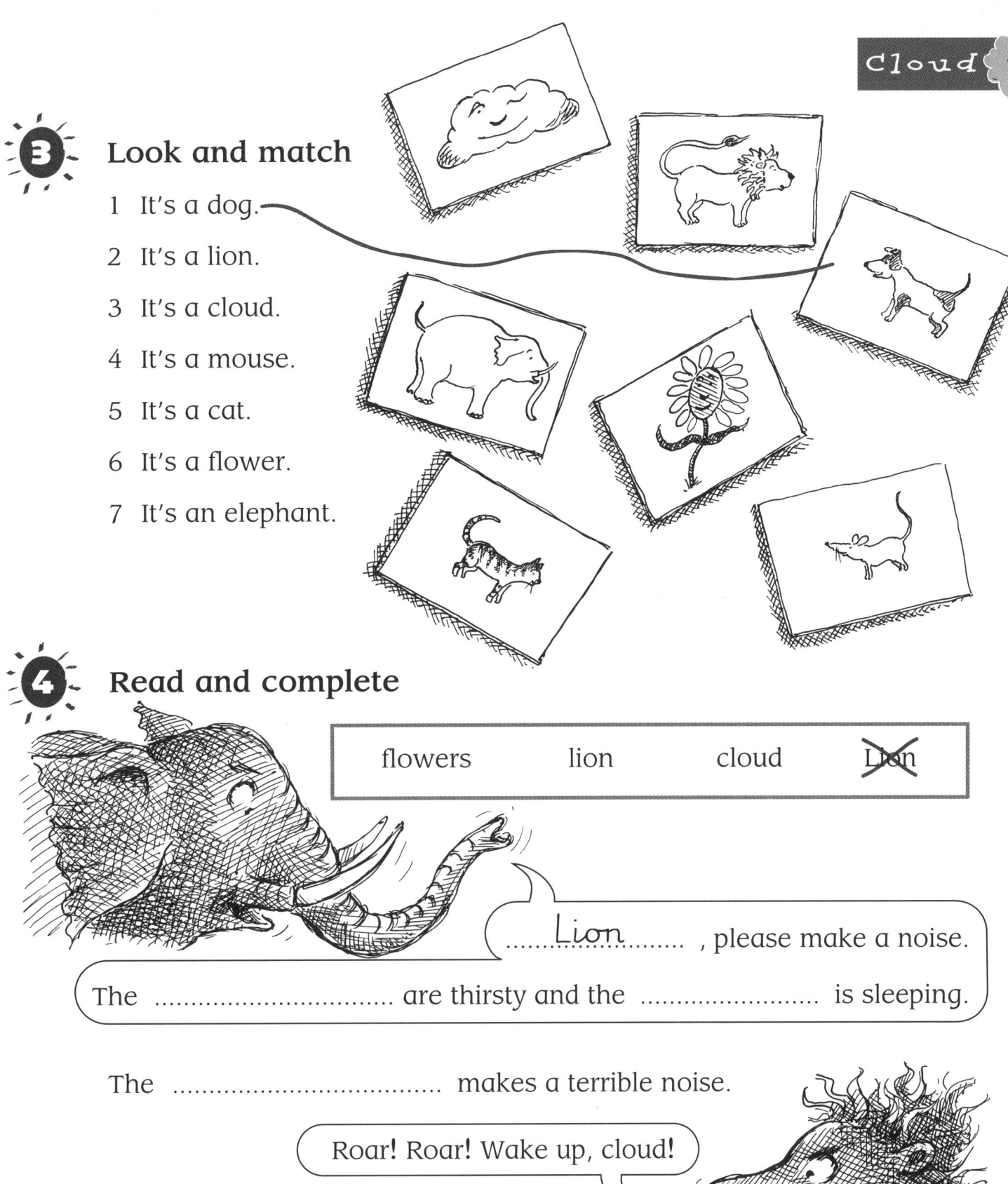

3 **Look and match**

1 It's a dog.

2 It's a lion.

3 It's a cloud.

4 It's a mouse.

5 It's a cat.

6 It's a flower.

7 It's an elephant.

4 **Read and complete**

| flowers | lion | cloud | ~~Lion~~ |

...........Lion........... , please make a noise.

The .... are thirsty and the .... is sleeping.

The .... makes a terrible noise.

Roar! Roar! Wake up, cloud!

But nothing happens.

5 **Act out the story**

Shorts and shoes

1 **Listen and colour**

1

2

2 **Classify the clothes**

shorts

trousers

sweater

t-shirt

shoes

tracksuit

shirt

coat

skirt

hat

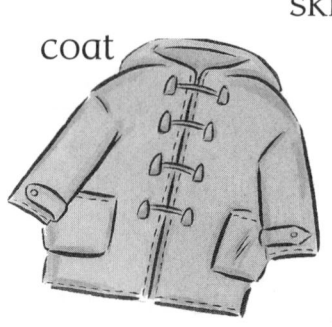

Clothes for cold weather ❄	Clothes for hot weather ☀
coat	

3 Draw and write

Draw and colour the clothes you are wearing today.

Write sentences.

Today I'm wearing a
white shirt and a
blue sweater.
I'm wearing

4 Answer the questions

Write Yes, I am or No, I'm not.

1 Are you wearing a white shirt? ....

2 Are you wearing black shoes? ....

3 Are you wearing a red sweater? ....

4 Are you wearing blue trousers? ....

5 Are you wearing a green skirt? ....

5 Listen and circle

What are Ted and Molly's favourite clothes?

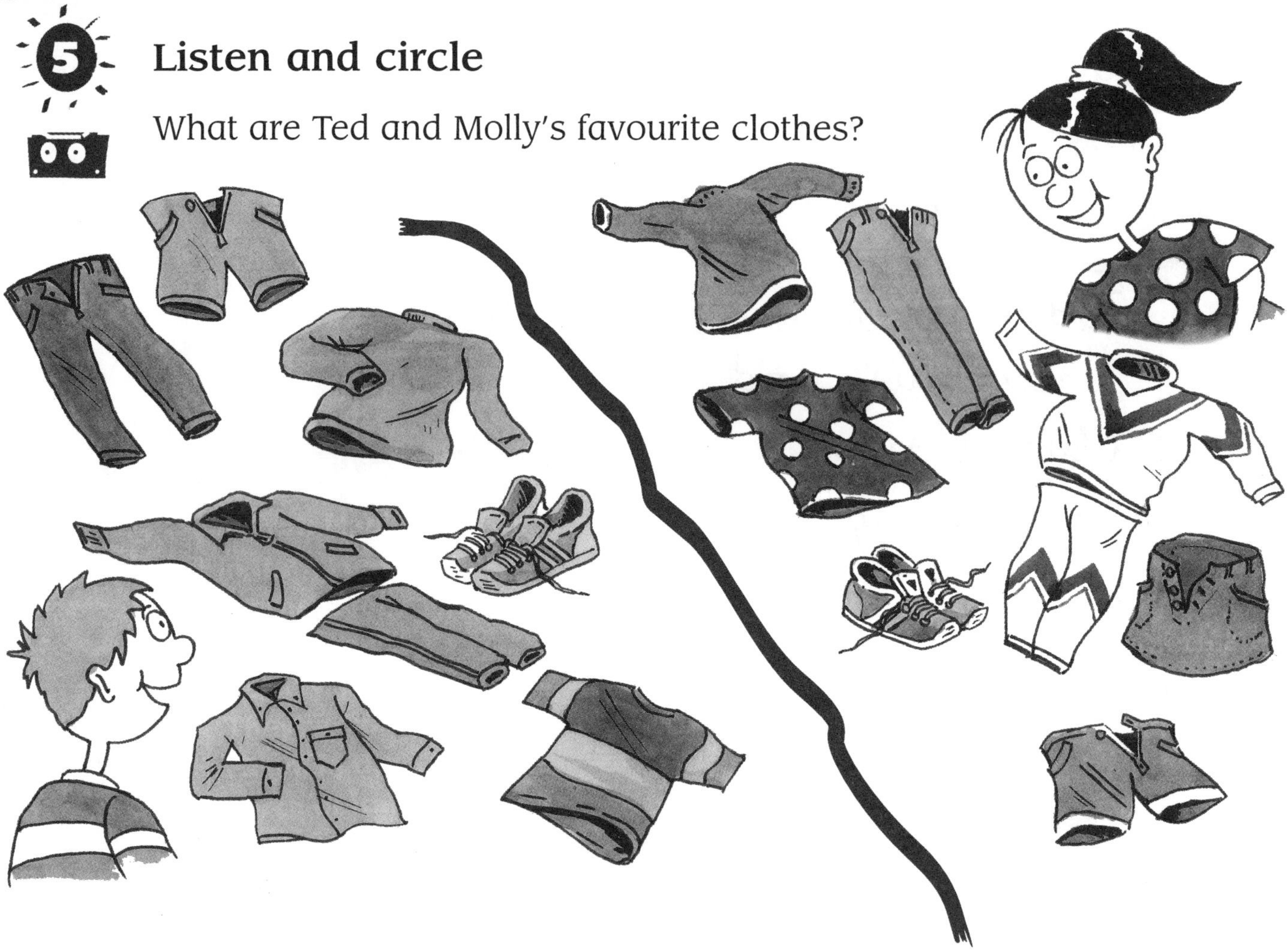

6 Write about your favourite clothes

My favourite clothes are ......*shorts and t-shirts*...... .

My favourite clothes are ....

Now find a partner.

What are your favourite clothes?

Shorts and t-shirts.

7 Listen and number

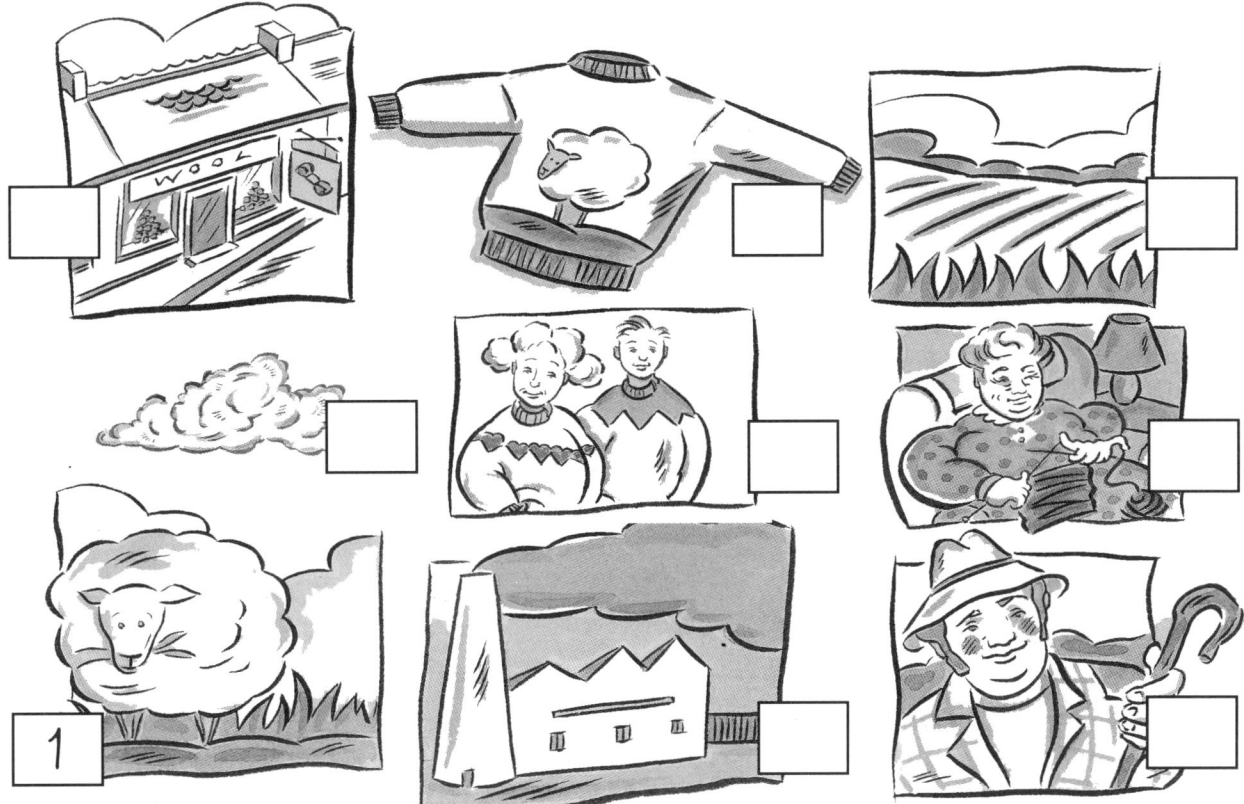

8 Design a t-shirt or sweater

Write about things you like.

Unit 7 is

Unit 8

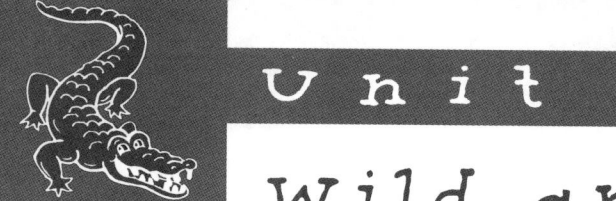

Wild animals

1 Look and match

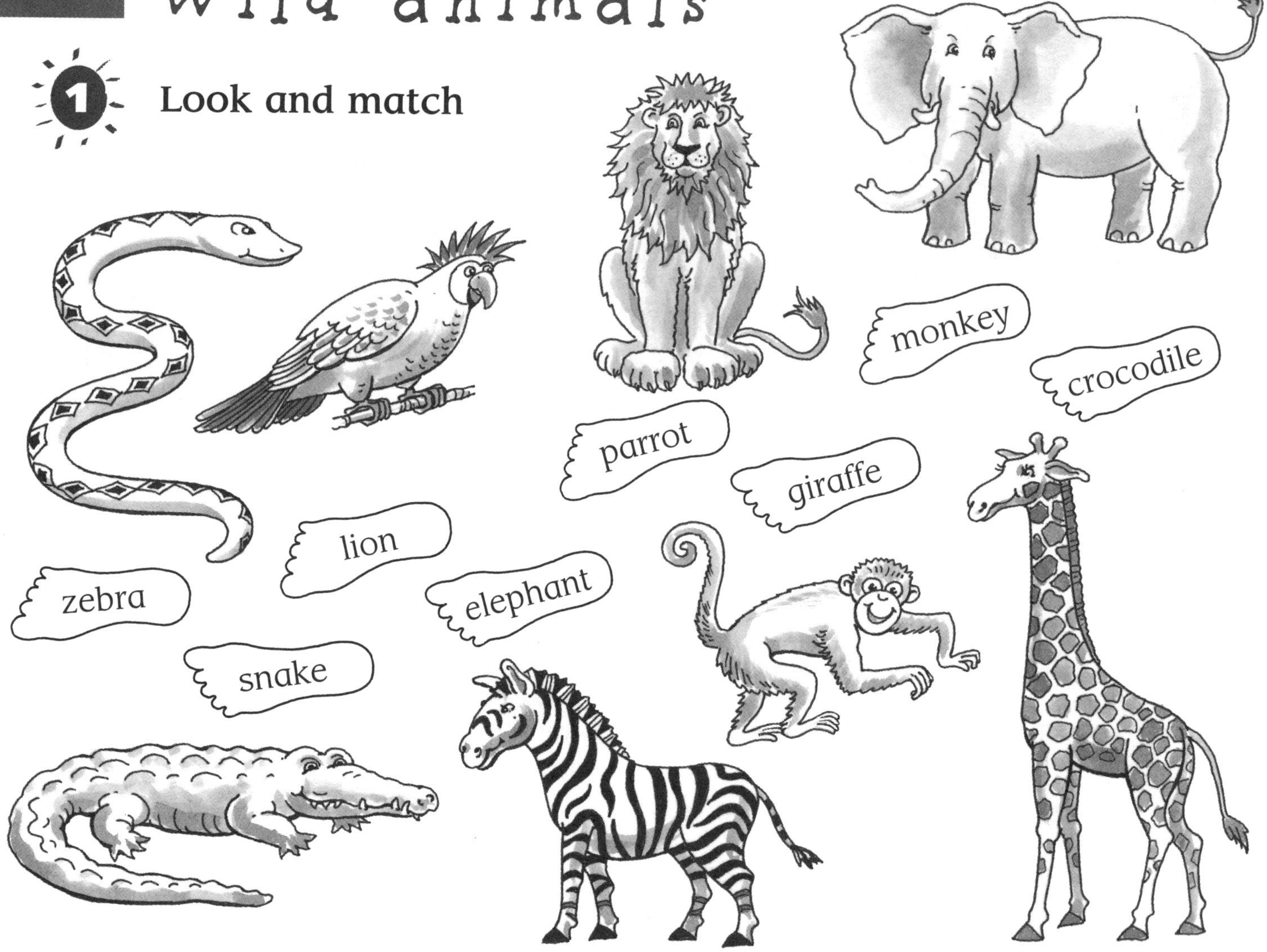

monkey
crocodile
parrot
giraffe
lion
zebra
elephant
snake

2 Classify the animals

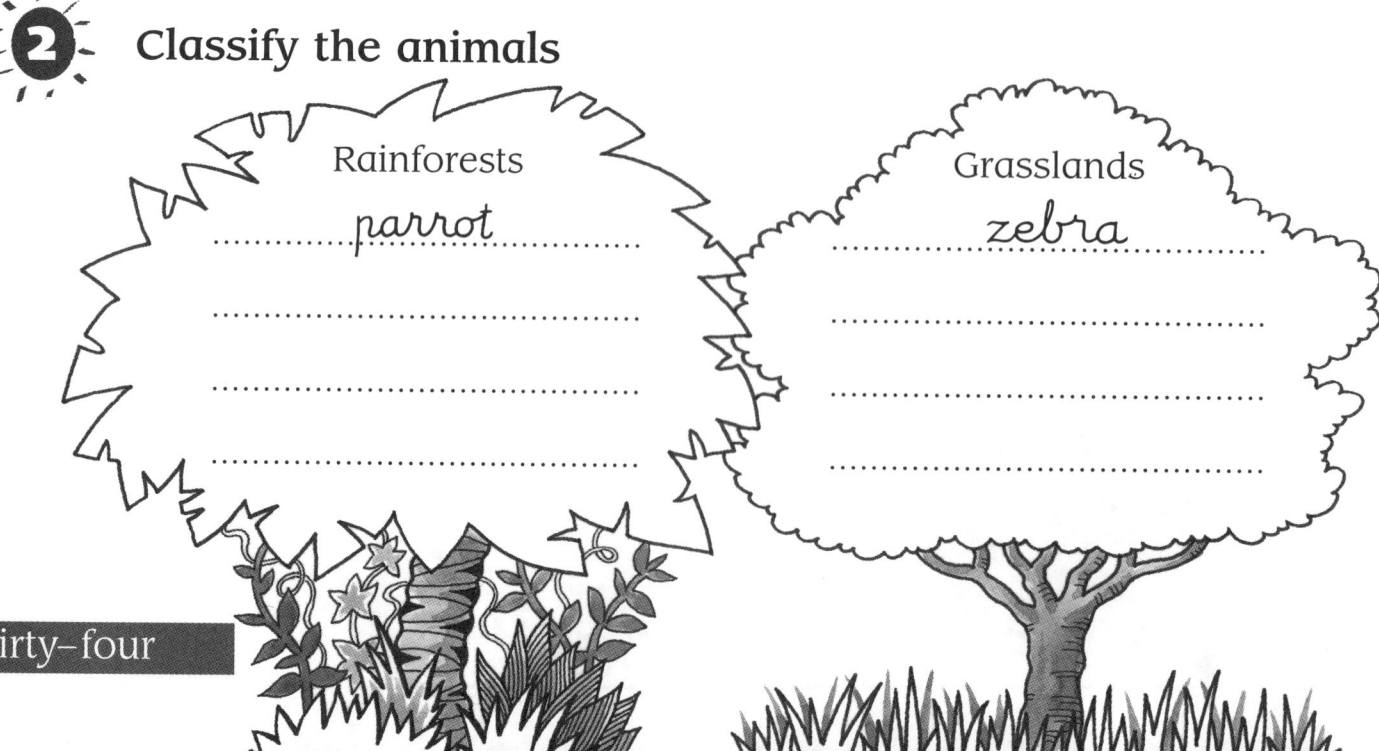

Rainforests
parrot
Grasslands
zebra

 **Look and write**

on   in   behind   under

1 Where's the ......*parrot*....... ?  It's ....*in*.......... the tree.

2 Where's the .... ?  It's .... the rock.

3 Where's the .... ?  It's .... the tree.

4 Where's the .... ?  It's .... Danny.

4 **Invent your dream story**

We're walking in the ....

We can't see the animals.

Where's the .... ?

.... ?

Oh, look! It's .... !

8

5. Answer the questions

1   Where's the lion? It's .....*in the pencil case*..... .

2   Where's the parrot? It's ....

3   Where's the elephant? It's ....

4   Where's the monkey? It's ....

6. Draw and write

Hide wild animals in the classroom!

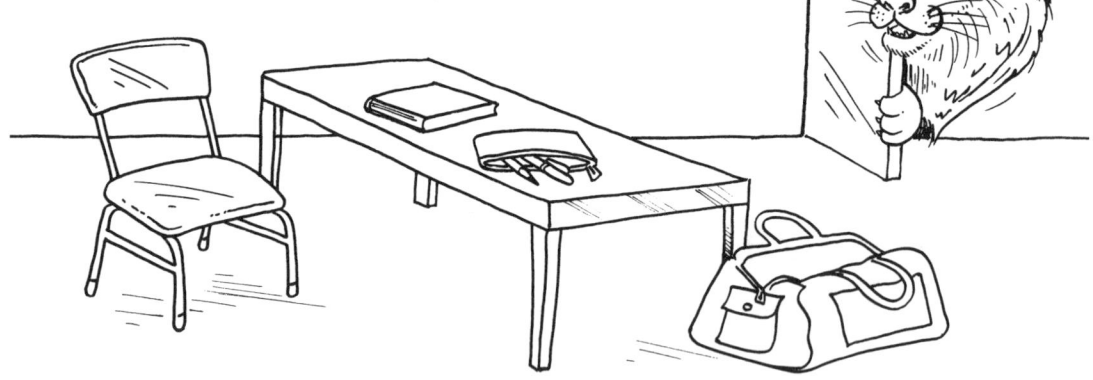

.....*A lion is behind the door*.....................................

....

....

....

....

7 Play a guessing game

Have you got a monkey in your classroom?

Yes, I have.

Is it on the chair?

No, it isn't.

8 Write an animal riddle

Draw a picture of your animal.

I live in .....grasslands.......... .

I've got .....four legs.......... .

I'm .....black and white.......... .

What am I?

I live in ....

I've got ....

I'm ....

What am I?

Unit 8 is

1 Listen and number

 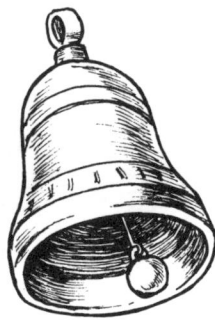  

[ ] [ ] [ ] [1] [ ]

2 Decorate the Christmas tree

Complete the sentences.

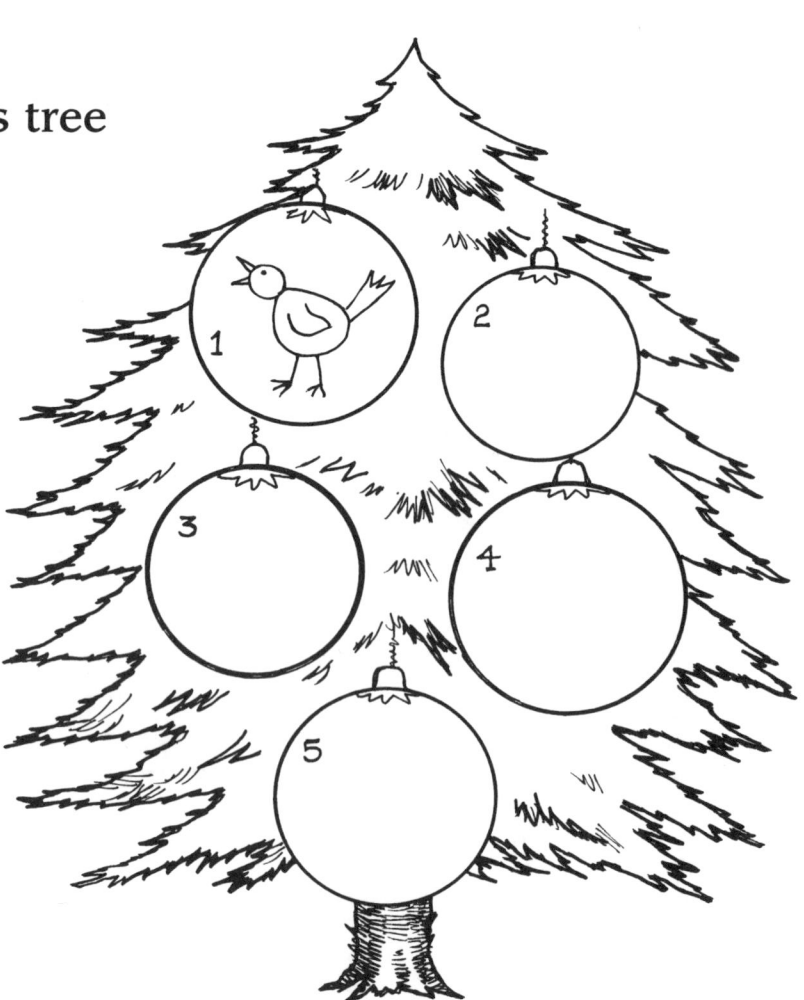

Number 1 is a ....bird........ .

Number 2 is a ....

Number 3 is a ....

Number 4 is a ....

Number 5 is a ....

 **1** **Complete the rhyme**

| egg | Easter | ~~Five~~ | rabbits |

...... *Five* ...... little ....

On .... Day

One finds an ....

And runs away

2 **Find the eggs**

Colour the small eggs blue.
Colour the big eggs red.
Colour the eggs with stars yellow.

Now look and count.

How many small eggs? ...... *eleven* ....

How many big eggs? ....

How many eggs with stars? ....

Extra activities

1 Colour

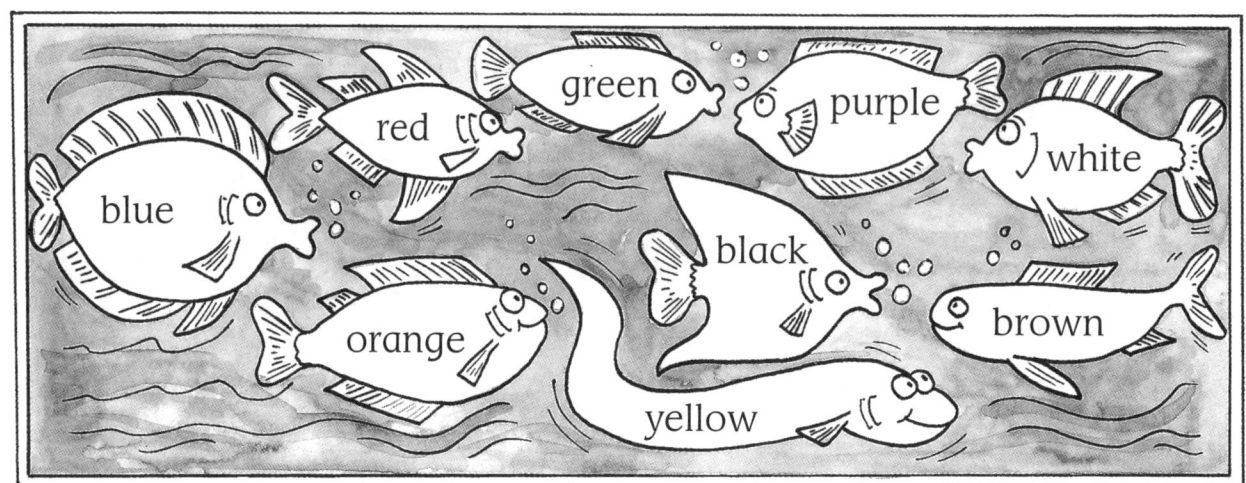

2 Match

| 1 | 2 | 3 | 4 | 5 |

bird   tree   egg   flower   fish

3 Write

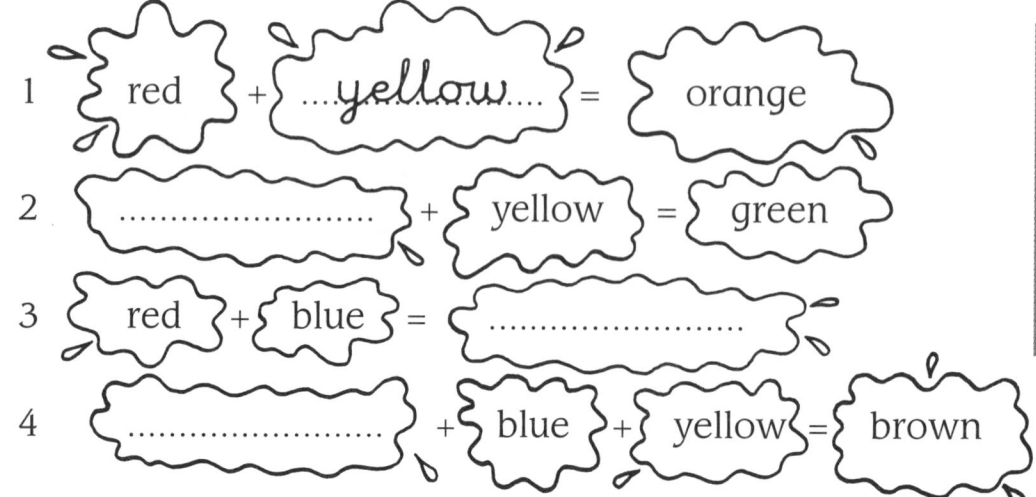

1   red + ...yellow.... = orange

2   .... + yellow = green

3   red + blue = ...

4   .... + blue + yellow = brown

blue
red
purple
~~yellow~~

4 Write

1 What colour is the fish?

..............red..............

2 What colour is the flower?

....

3 What colour is the tree?

....

4 What colour is the bird?

....

5 Match

1	What's your name?	Green.
2	What's your favourite colour?	I'm Molly.
3	What colour is the spinner?	No.
4	Is it blue?	Red and yellow.

6 Complete

1	red	yellow	blue	red	yellow	*blue*
2	orange	green	orange	green	orange	....
3	blue	black	black	blue	black	....
4	brown	white	purple	brown	white	....

Unit 2

Extra activities

1 **Draw**

five
two
three
one
four
six
ten
seven
nine
eight

It's a ....

2 **Count and write**

four ....

....

3 **Match**

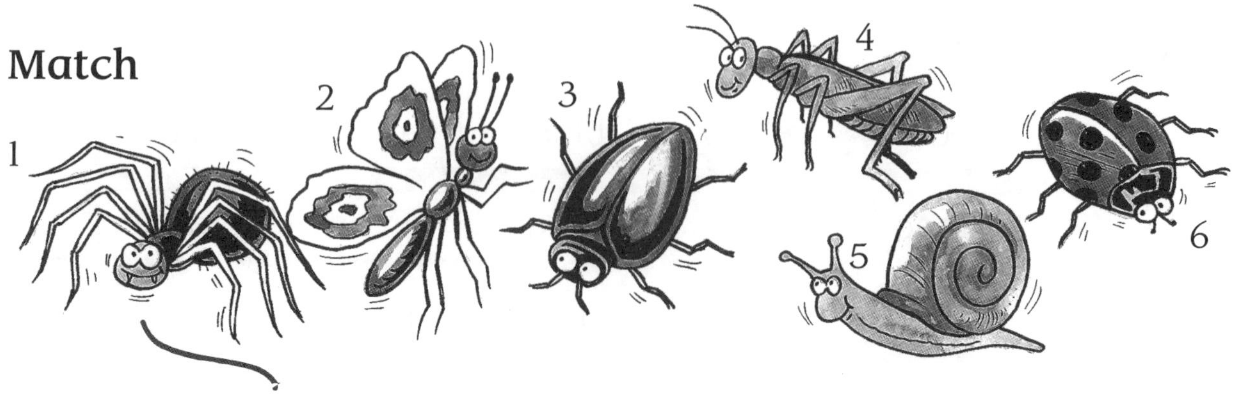

1   2   3   4   5   6

butterfly   spider   grasshopper   snail   beetle   ladybird

4 Complete

1 Snails have got ....no........ legs.

2 Ladybirds have got .... legs.

3 Beetles have got .... legs.

4 Butterflies have got .... legs.

5 Spiders have got .... legs.

6 Grasshoppers have got .... legs.

5 Write

| I'm eight. | I'm Sally. | ~~Hello.~~ | Sorry. Not now. |

Sally: ....Hello...............

Danny: Hello. What's your name?

Sally: ....

Danny: How old are you?

Sally: ....

Danny: Come and play with me.

Sally: ....

Danny: Goodbye.

6 Match

run   jump   walk   crawl   fly

Extra activities

1 Complete

	p
	e
	n

2 Count and write

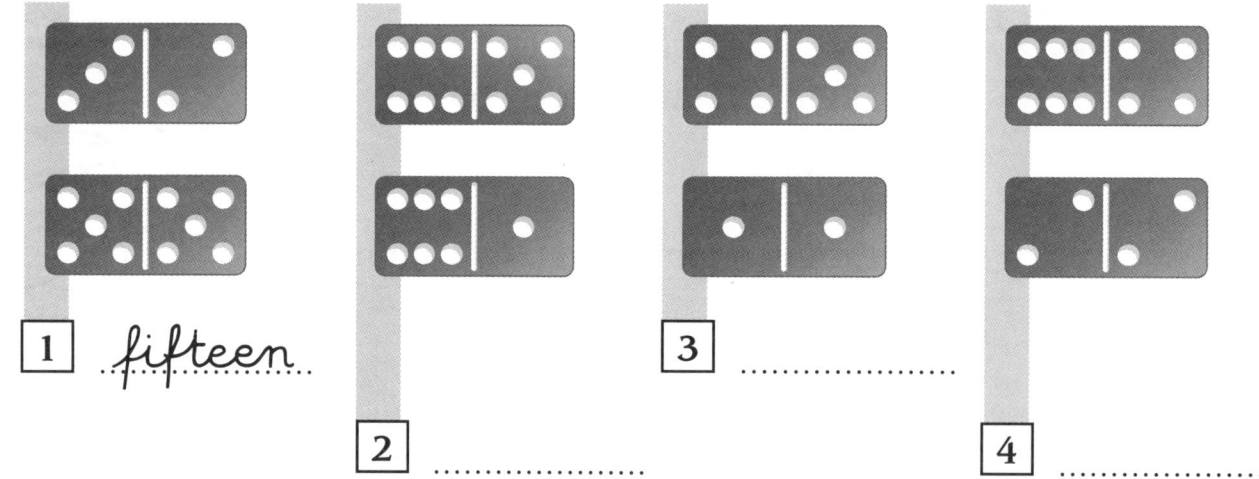

1 .fifteen.

2 ....

3 ....

4 ....

3 Write

1 What's this? c n p e i l

It's a ....pencil........ .

2 What's this? b r b r e u

It's a ....

3 What's this? k o b o

It's a ....

4 What's this? u e l r r

It's a ....

4 Look and complete

1 How much is *the rubber* ? Ten pence.

2 How much is .... ? Sixteen pence.

3 How .... ? Twelve pence.

4 How .... ? Twenty pence.

5 Write

| 20p.   Goodbye.   ~~Hello.~~   Thank you.   Goodbye. |
| Here you are.   How much is the ruler, please?   Hello. |

You: ....*Hello*...........................

Shopkeeper: ....

You: ....

Shopkeeper: ....

You: ....

Shopkeeper: ....

You: ....

Shopkeeper: ....

6 Count and write

1 ....*twelve*.... pence

2 .... pence

3 .... pence

Unit 4

Extra activities

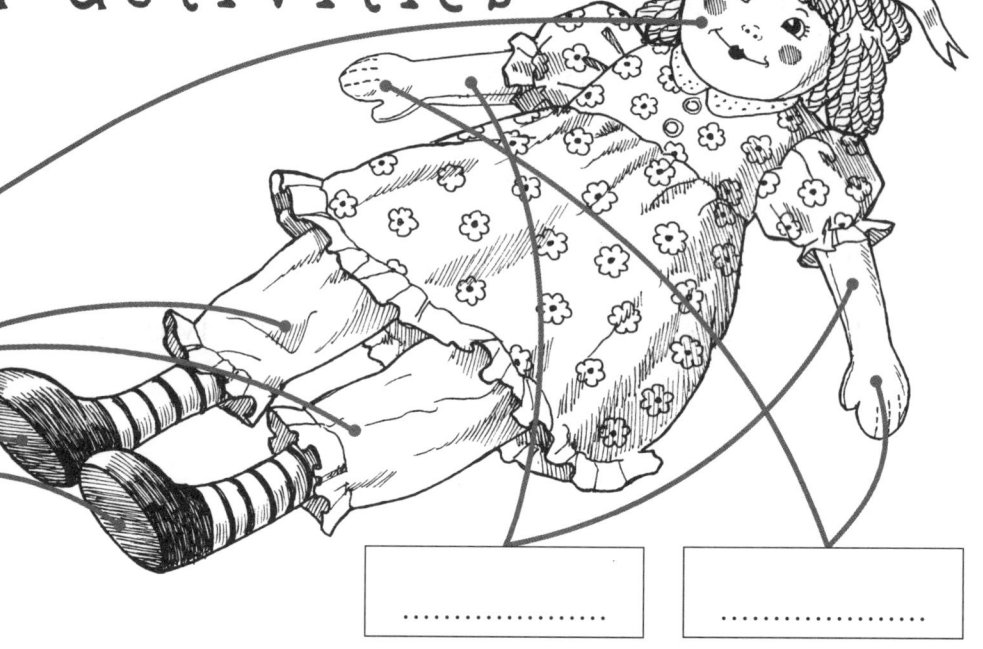

1 Write

head

....

....

....

2 Match

1

2

I've got big eyes.

I've got a small nose.

I've got small ears.

I've got big hands.

3

4

3 Read and circle

1 Tom has got big eyes.   Yes   No

2 Rosa has got small ears.   Yes   No

3 Tom has got a small nose.   Yes   No

4 Rosa has got big eyes.   Yes   No

5 Tom has got big ears.   Yes   No

6 Rosa has got a small mouth.   Yes   No

 **Draw and write**

Hello, I'm Sally. I've got big eyes and small ears. I've got a small nose and a small mouth. I've got black hair.

Hello, I'm ....
I've got ....
I've got ....
I've got ....

 **Colour and complete**

The scarecrow has got a .....red......... head,

.... arms and .... legs.

He's got .... hands

and .... feet.

 **Write about a friend**

Jenny is my friend. She's got big eyes and small ears. She's got a small nose and a small mouth. She's got black hair.

.... is my friend. ....

....

....

Extra activities

1 Find and write

1 g*randmother*
2 g.........................
3 m.........................
4 f.........................
5 b.........................
6 s.........................
7 d.........................
8 c.........................

g	r	a	n	d	m	o	t	h	e	r
h	i	b	u	c	o	k	a	d	e	t
a	s	s	i	s	t	e	r	o	h	a
r	b	r	o	t	h	e	r	g	s	f
w	t	p	m	f	e	b	g	a	i	a
j	c	a	t	b	r	l	o	c	s	t
m	a	g	e	m	u	b	f	u	t	h
i	t	n	t	c	d	l	y	e	r	e
g	r	a	n	d	f	a	t	h	e	r

2 Read and circle

1 I've got two sisters and a cat.

2 I've got three brothers.

3 I've got two brothers and a dog.

4 I've got one brother and one sister.

3 Complete

	Me	My brother	My sister	My mother	My father
Colour of hair					
Colour of eyes					

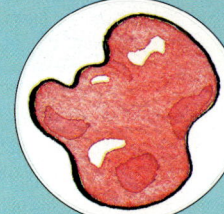

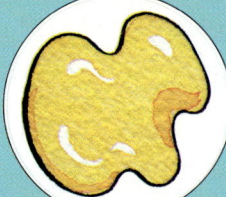

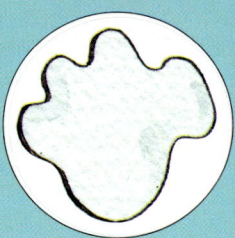

one	two	three
four	five	six

seven	eight	nine	ten

6

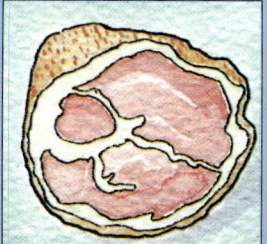   

    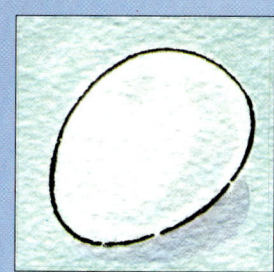

7

11 12 13 14 15 16

3

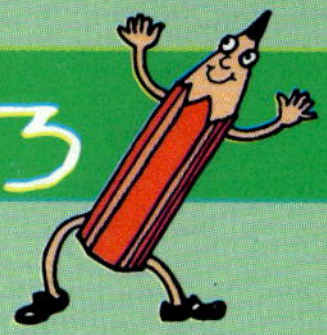

17 18

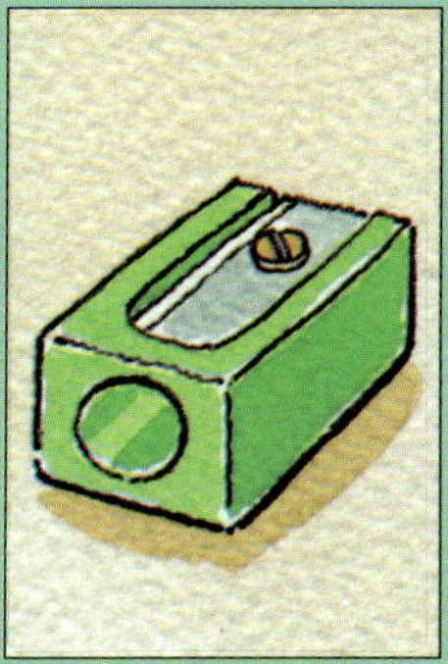
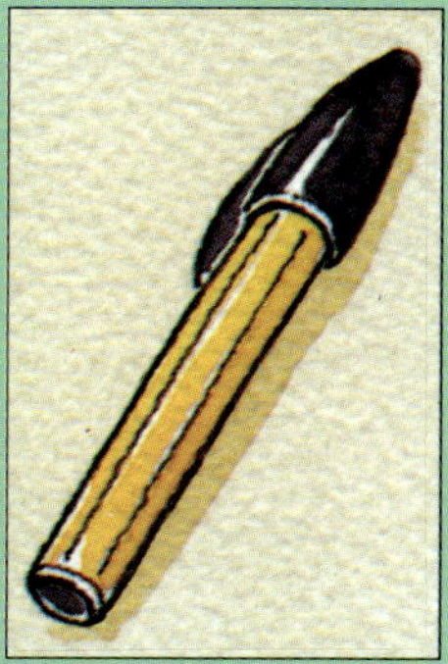
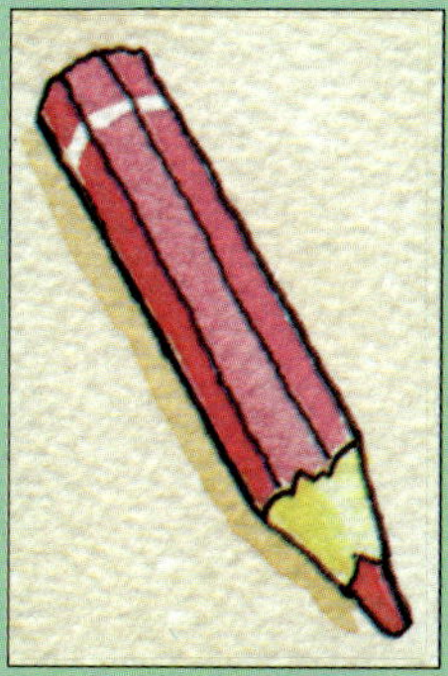
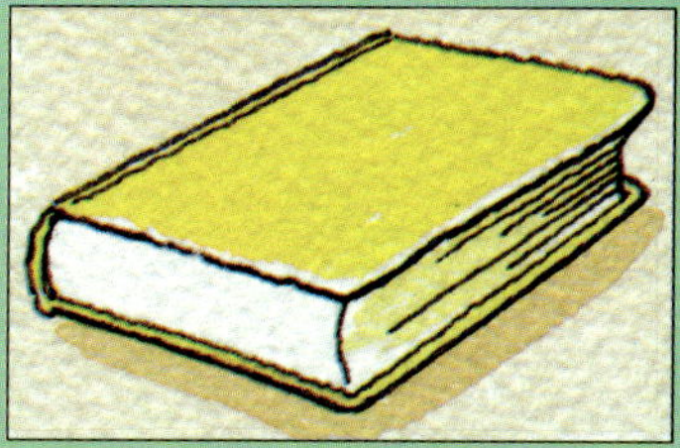

19 20

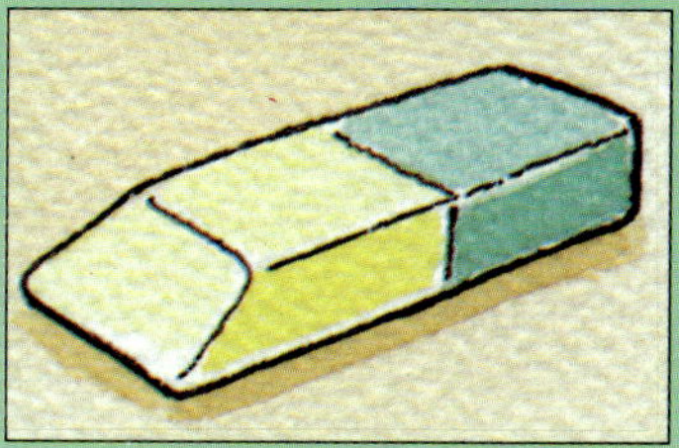
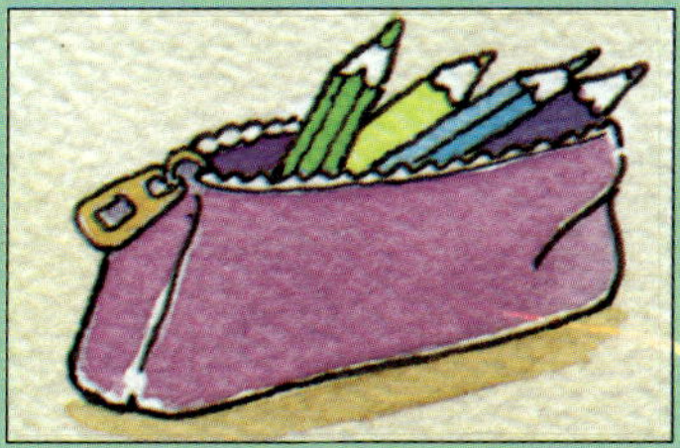
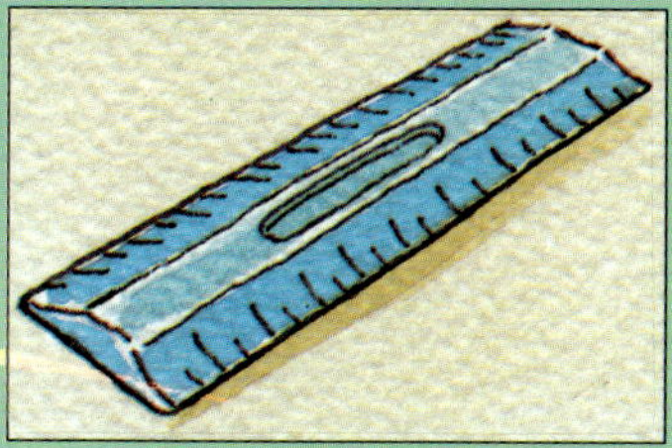

4

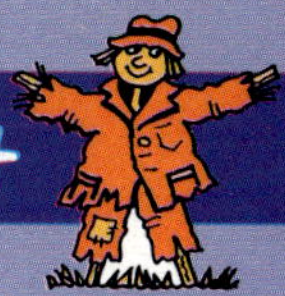

leg	mouth	eye	head		
hair	ear	nose	arm	hand	feet

5

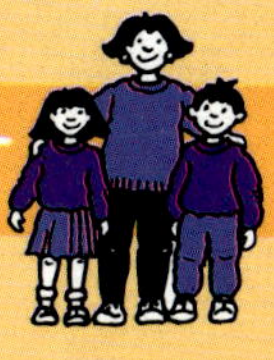

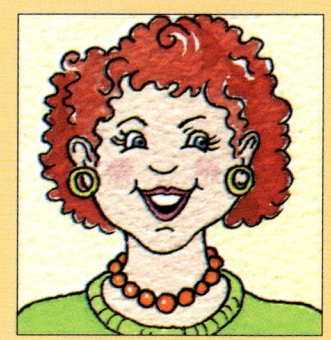

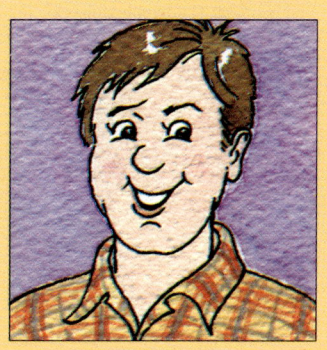

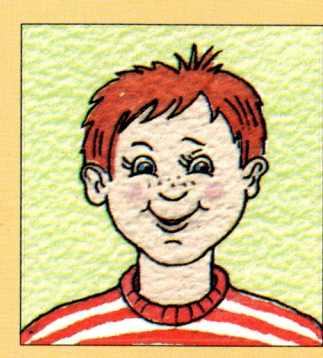

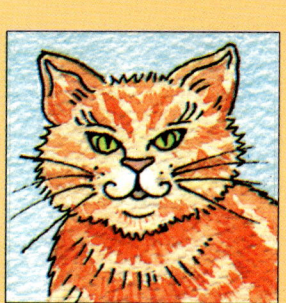

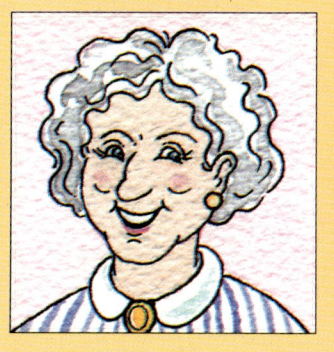

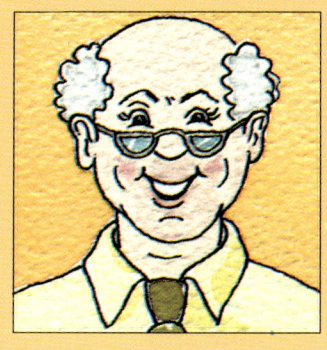

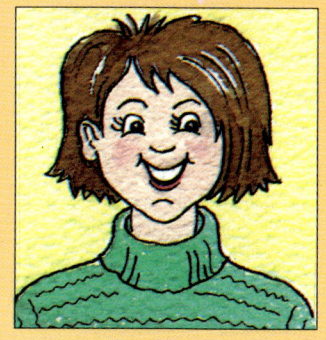

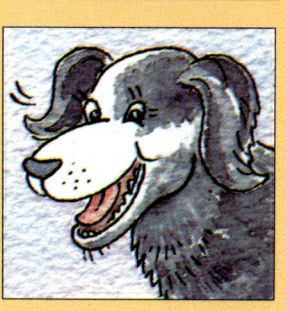

4 Write Yes I have or No, I haven't.

1 Have you got a dog? ....

2 Have you got brown eyes? ....

3 Have you got big feet? ....

4 Have you got a cat? ....

5 Have you got fair hair? ....

5 Read and circle

Use crayons.

family words = black
parts of the body = blue

grandfather

father

nose   ears   eyes   hands

mouth

legs   grandmother

mother   arms   brother   head   hair   sister

teeth

6 Write sentences

1 sister / got / My / big / has / eyes

...My sister has got big eyes...........

2 hair / I've / black / got

....

3 brothers / got / two / I've / a / cat / and

....

4 dog / ears / got / big / My / has

....

Extra activities

1 Complete

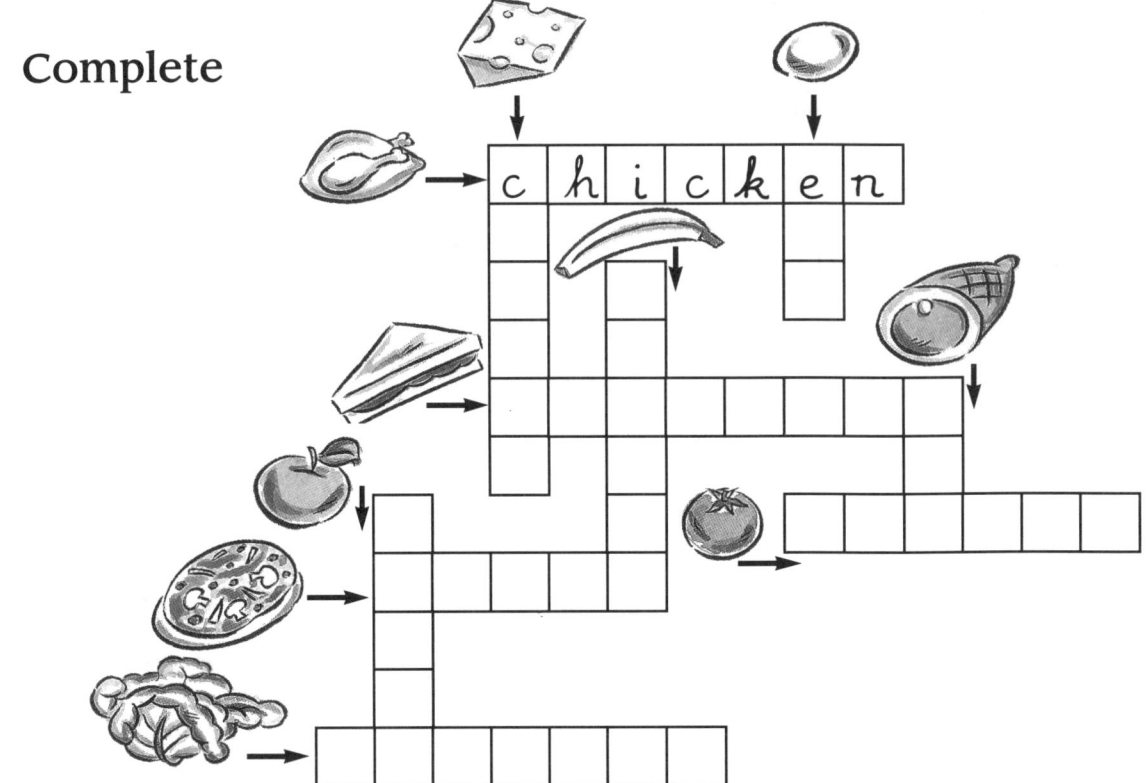

c h i c k e n

2 Write *Yes, I do* **or** *No, I don't.*

1 Do you like tomatoes? ....

2 Do you like hamburgers? ....

3 Do you like apples? ....

4 Do you like eggs? ....

3  **Read and circle**

Use crayons.

food from animals = red
food from plants = green

ham   apple   banana   egg   lettuce

cheese   tomato   chicken   carrot

4 Write

I like ....ham sandwiches.... .   I like ....

I don't like *cheese sandwiches* .   I don't like ....

5 Complete

	I like	I don't like
colours		
food		
animals		

6 Read and match

1 Danny plants a seed.

2 A tiny plant grows.

3 Danny waters the plant.

4 A flower grows.

Unit 7

Extra activities

1 Complete

1 <u>t</u> - <u>s</u> <u>h</u> irt

2 _ _ ousers

3 sh _ _ ts

4 sk _ _ t

5 _ _ oes

6 c _ _ t

7 _ weat _ _

8 _ _ acksuit

9 _ at

10 _ _ irt

2 Read and colour

I'm wearing blue trousers, a red t-shirt and black shoes.

I'm wearing a green skirt, a yellow sweater and blue shoes.

3 Write about your clothes

I like my _red t-shirt_ .   I don't like my _blue shoes_ .

I like my ....   I don't like my ....

I ....   I ....

I ....   I ....

 **Write**

1 What colour is your favourite sweater? ....

2 What colour is your favourite t-shirt? ....

3 What colour is your favourite tracksuit? ....

4 What colour are your favourite trousers? ....

5 What colour are your favourite shoes? ....

Match

1

2

3

4

5

6

sheep

farmer

wool

factory

shop

sweater

 **Read and circle**

1 Sweaters are for cold weather.   (Yes)   No

2 Shorts are for cold weather.   Yes   No

3 Cotton t-shirts are for hot weather.   Yes   No

4 Coats are for hot weather.   Yes   No

5 Wool trousers are for cold weather.   Yes   No

Unit 8

Extra activities

1 Find and write

1 lion.................... 5 p.....................

2 g..................... 6 c.....................

3 m..................... 7 z.....................

4 e..................... 8 s.....................

c	r	o	c	o	d	i	l	e
t	f	a	l	j	o	g	e	l
p	r	g	i	r	a	f	f	e
a	c	m	o	n	z	o	l	p
r	m	o	n	k	e	y	u	h
r	e	p	s	a	b	m	d	a
o	k	l	w	p	r	h	u	n
t	b	r	s	n	a	k	e	t

2 Read and circle

1 Lions live in grasslands.   Yes   No

2 Crocodiles live in grasslands.   Yes   No

3 Zebras live in rainforests.   Yes   No

4 Parrots live in rainforests.   Yes   No

3 Complete

1 Where's the ....parrot.... ? It's .....in..... the tree.

2 Where's the .... ? It's .... the tree.

3 Where's the ...monkey... ? It's .... the rock

4 Where's the .... ? It's .... the rock

4 Look and write

A monkey is on the table..........

....

....

....

5 Complete and match

I'm very tall.

I'm a ....giraffe...... .

I like bananas.

I'm a ....

I've got a big mouth.

I'm a ....

I've got big ears.

I'm an ....

6 Read and write

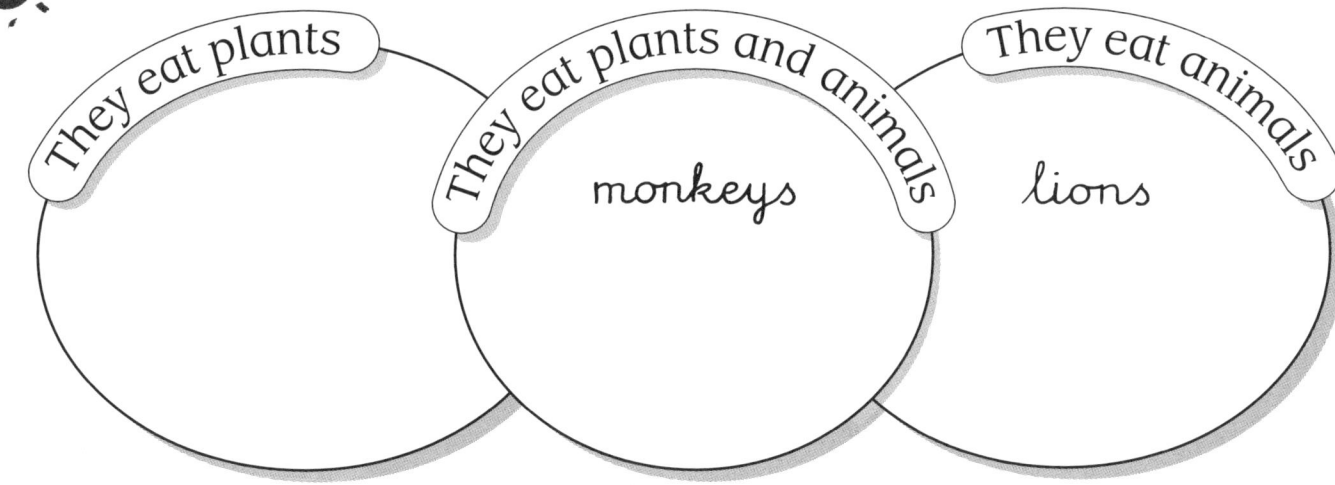

They eat plants

They eat plants and animals

monkeys

They eat animals

lions

My Picture Dictionary

My Picture Dictionary

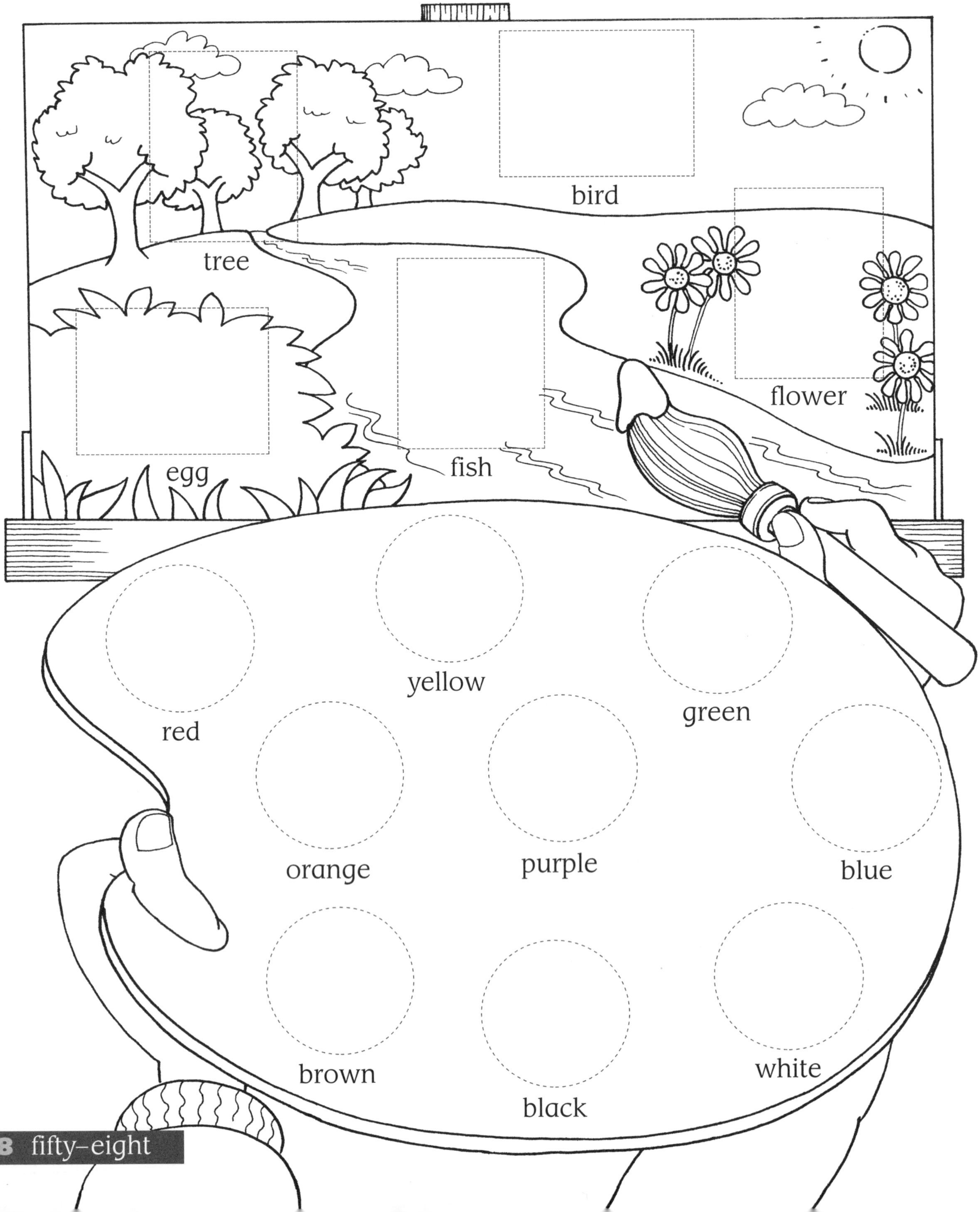

bird

tree

flower

egg

fish

yellow

green

red

orange

purple

blue

brown

white

black

My Picture Dictionary

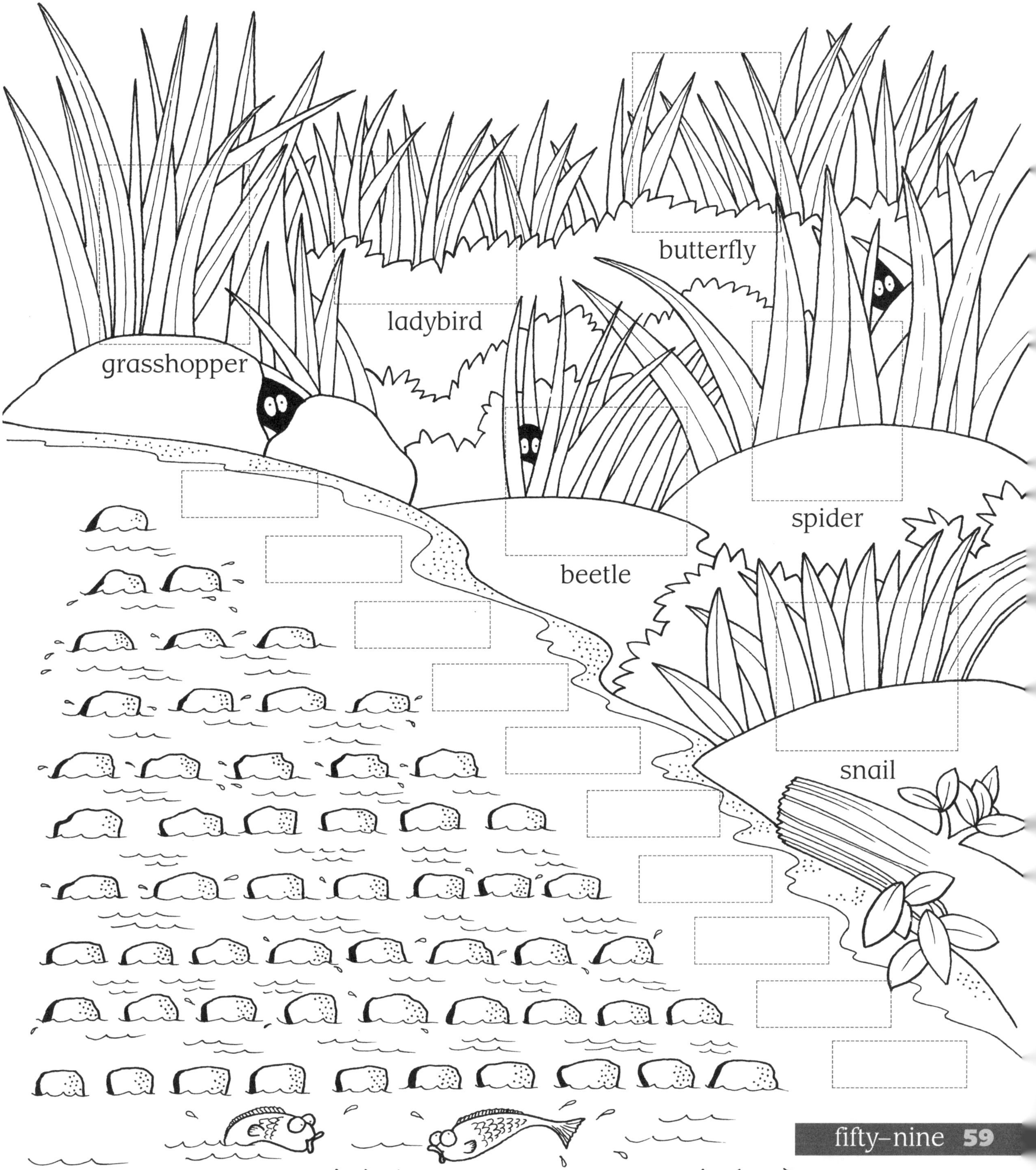

butterfly

ladybird

grasshopper

spider

beetle

snail

My Picture Dictionary

eleven   twelve   thirteen   fourteen   fifteen

sixteen   seventeen   eighteen   nineteen   twenty

pen

pencil
sharpener

rubber

pencil case   ruler   pencil   book

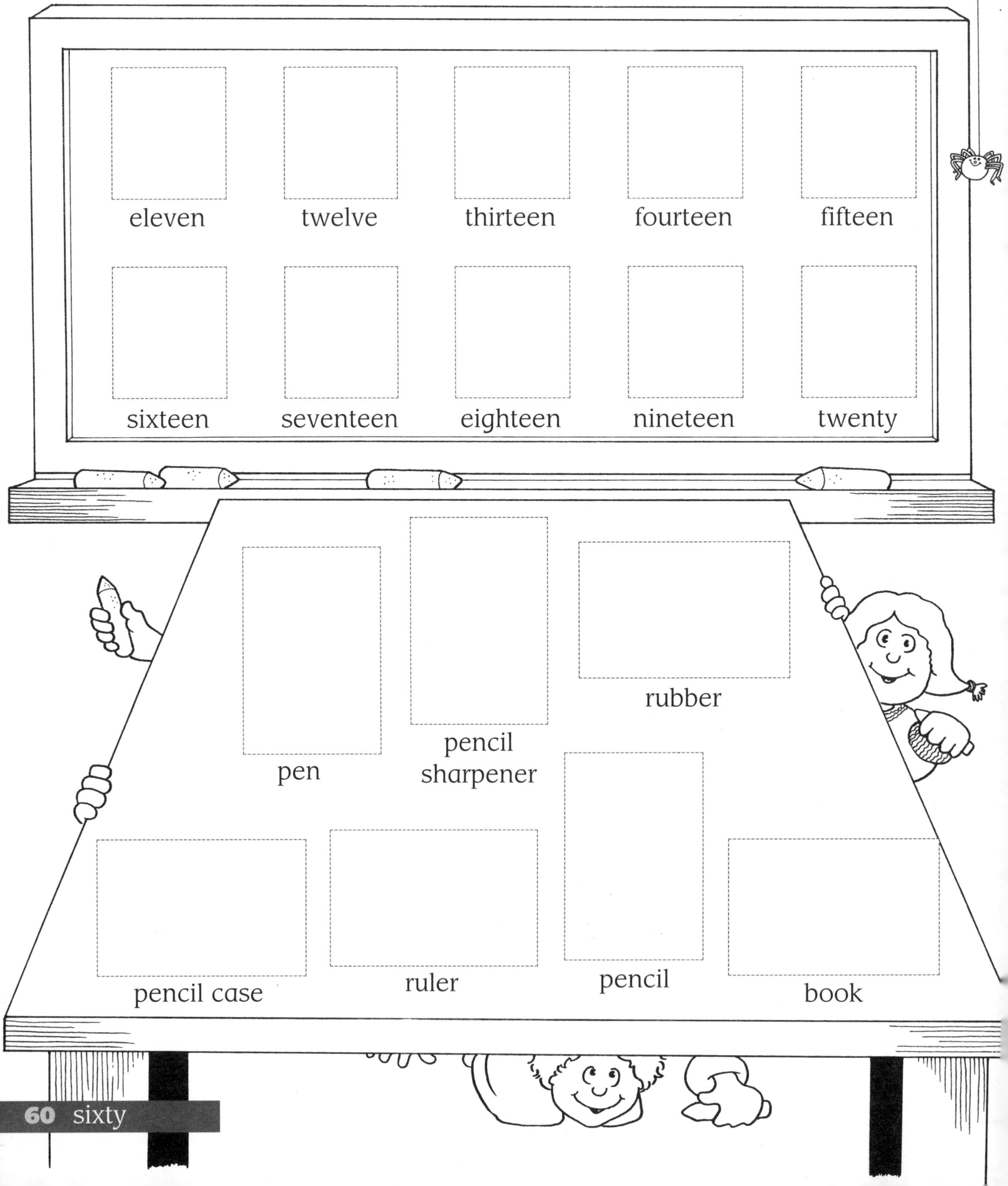

My Picture Dictionary

My Picture Dictionary

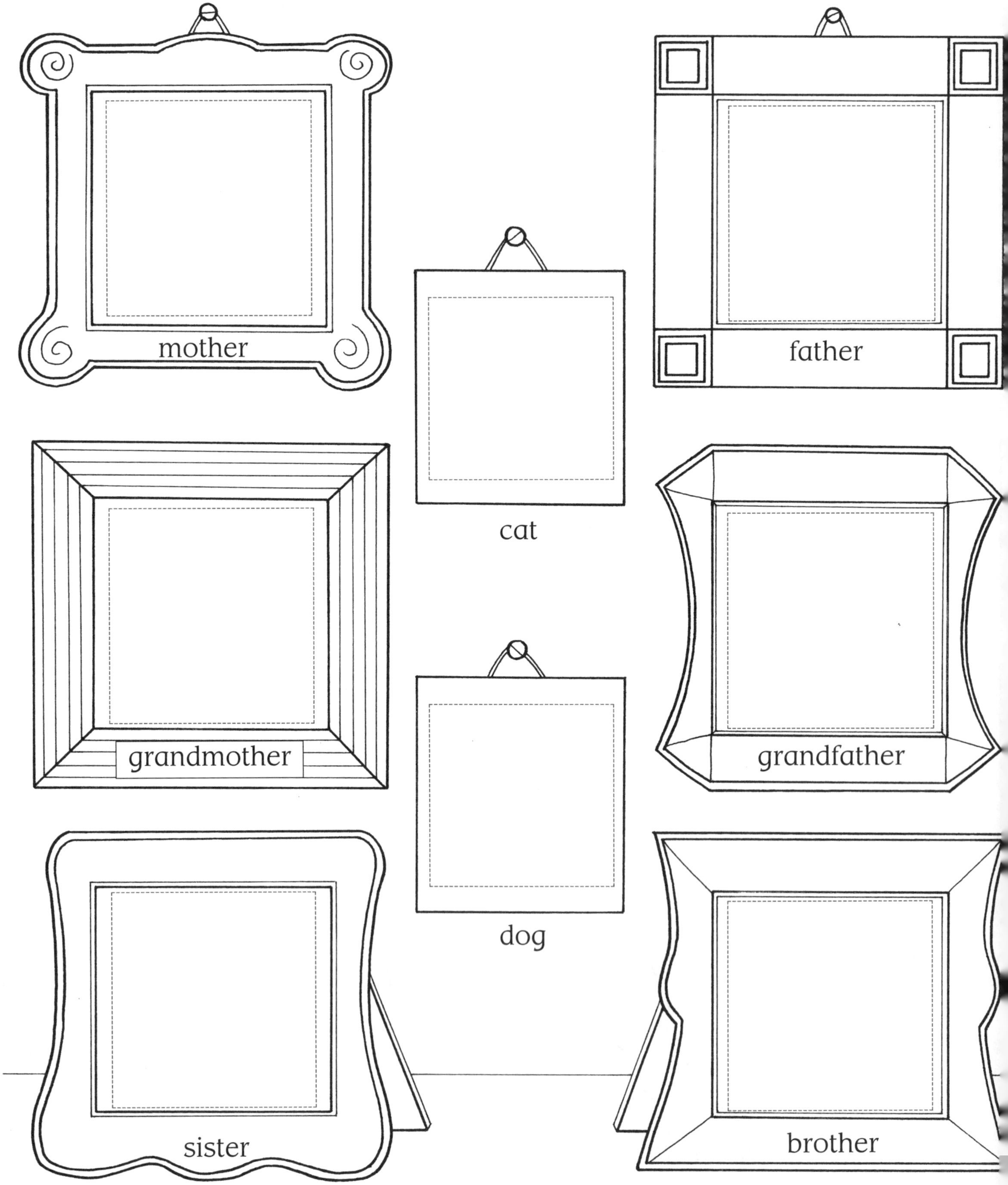

mother

cat

father

grandmother

dog

grandfather

sister

brother

My Picture Dictionary

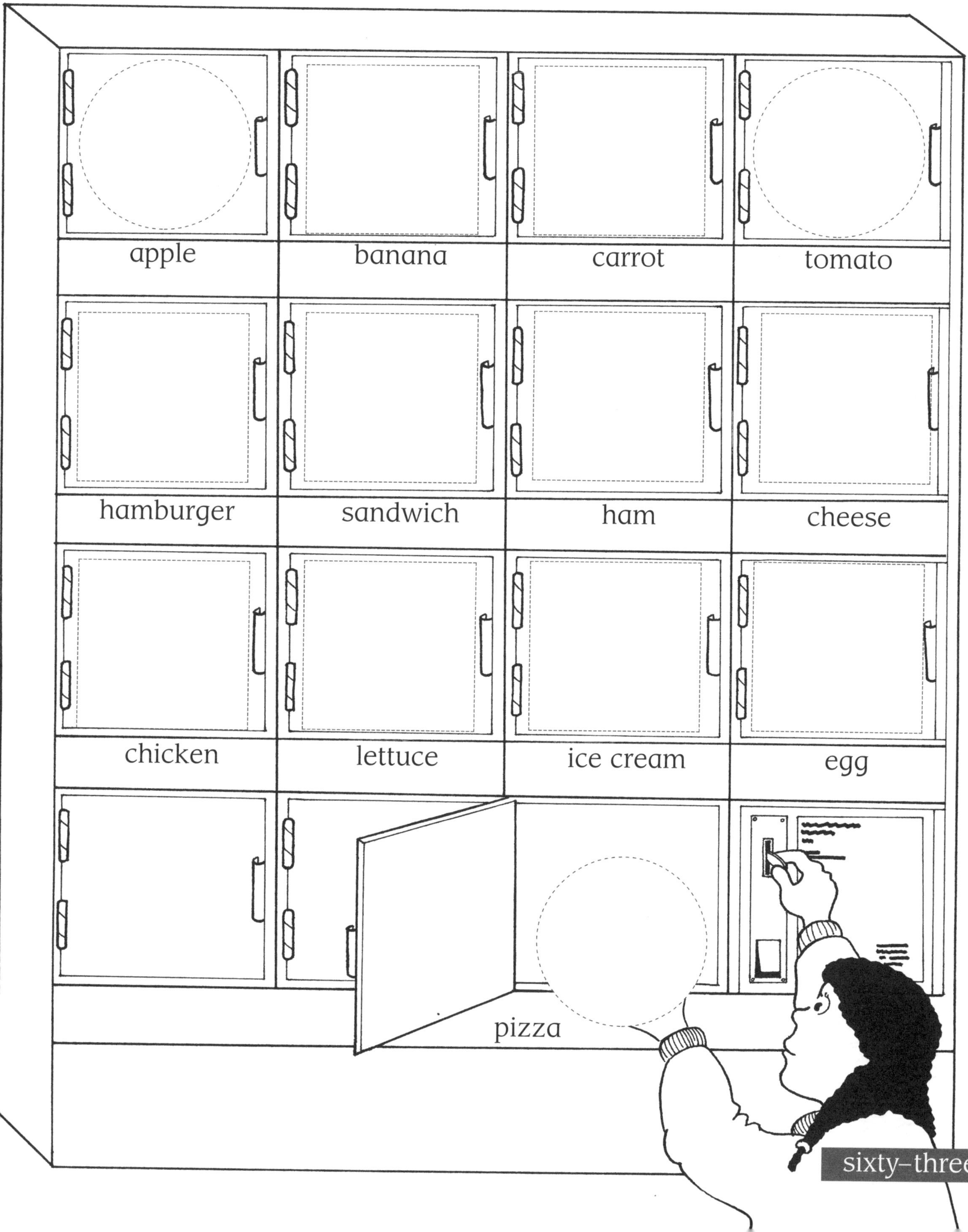

apple

banana

carrot

tomato

hamburger

sandwich

ham

cheese

chicken

lettuce

ice cream

egg

pizza

t-shirt

trousers

shorts

tracksuit

skirt

shirt

shoes

coat

hat

sweater

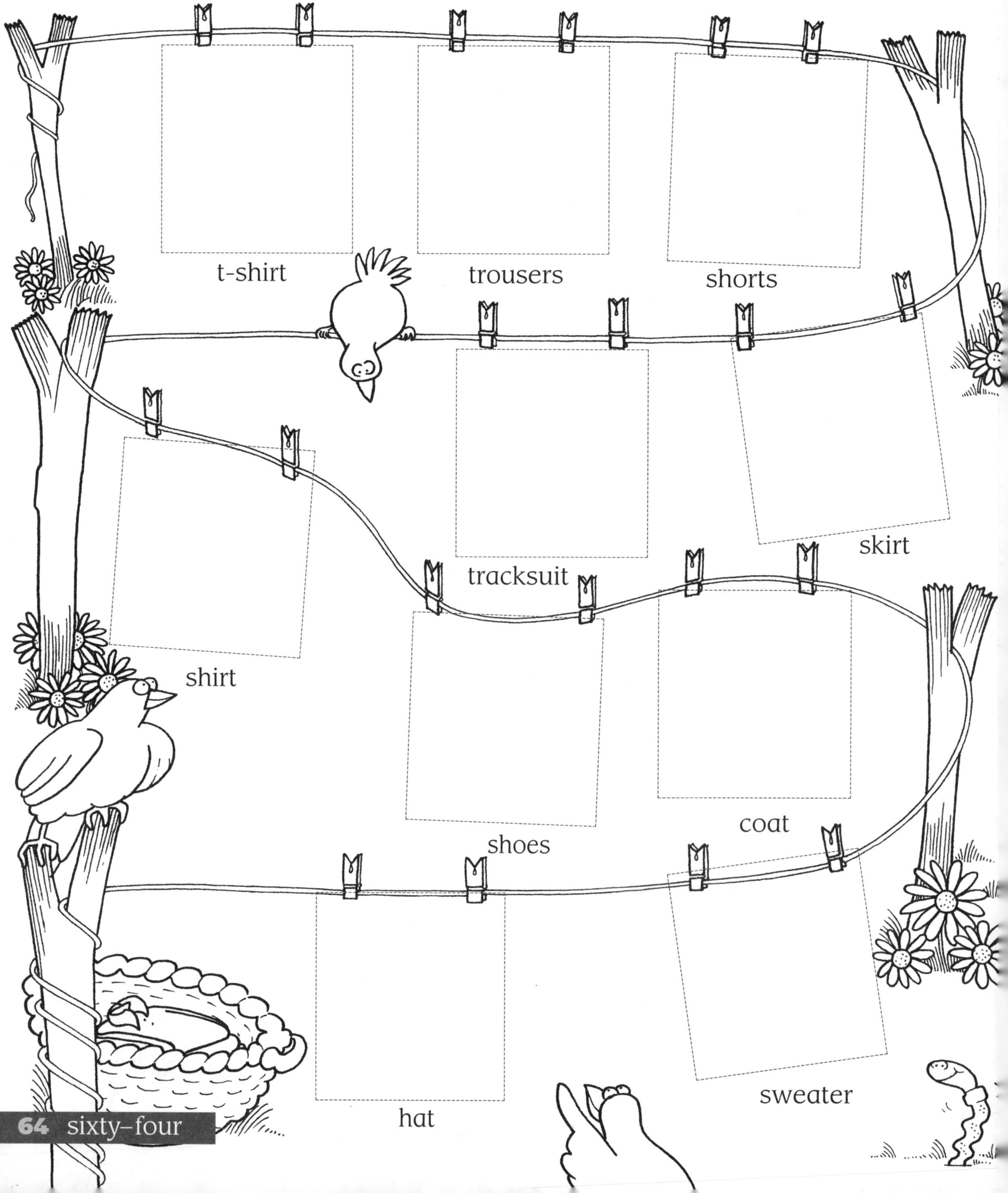

My Picture Dictionary

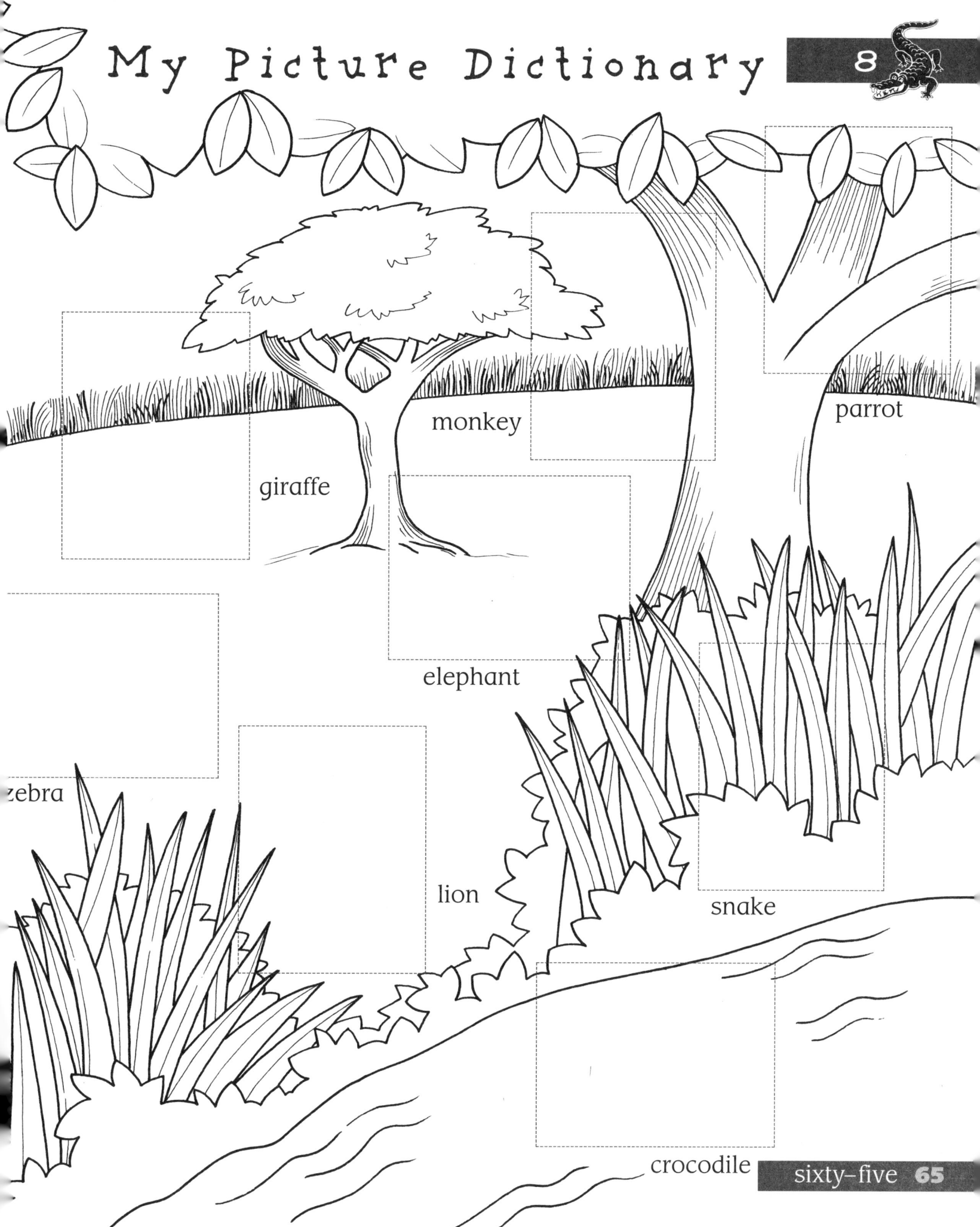

monkey

parrot

giraffe

elephant

zebra

lion

snake

crocodile

Cut Outs

Pencil puppets

Cut Outs

Colour spinner

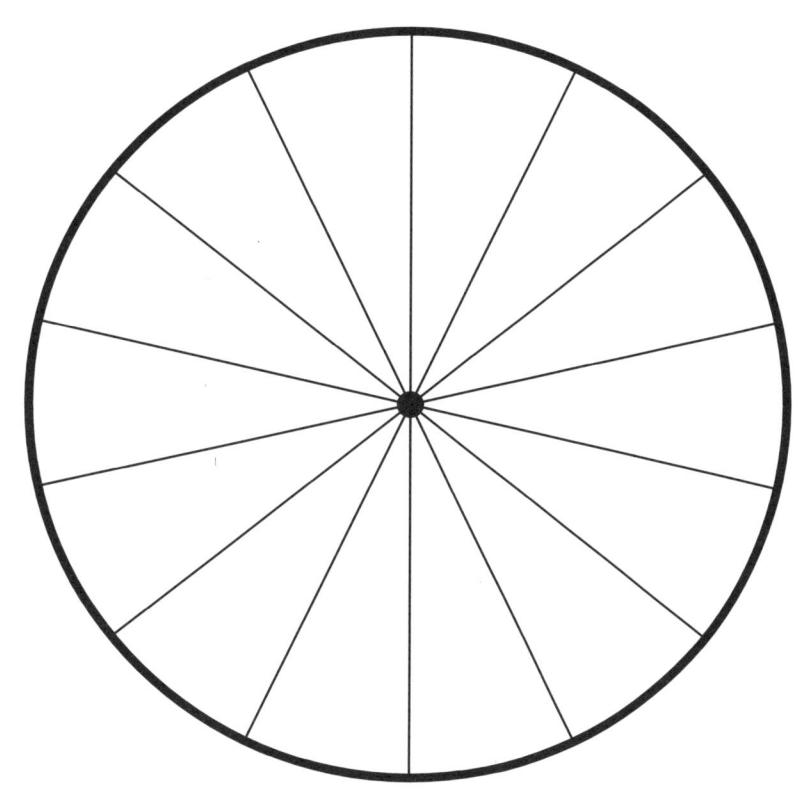

Cut Outs Two butterflies

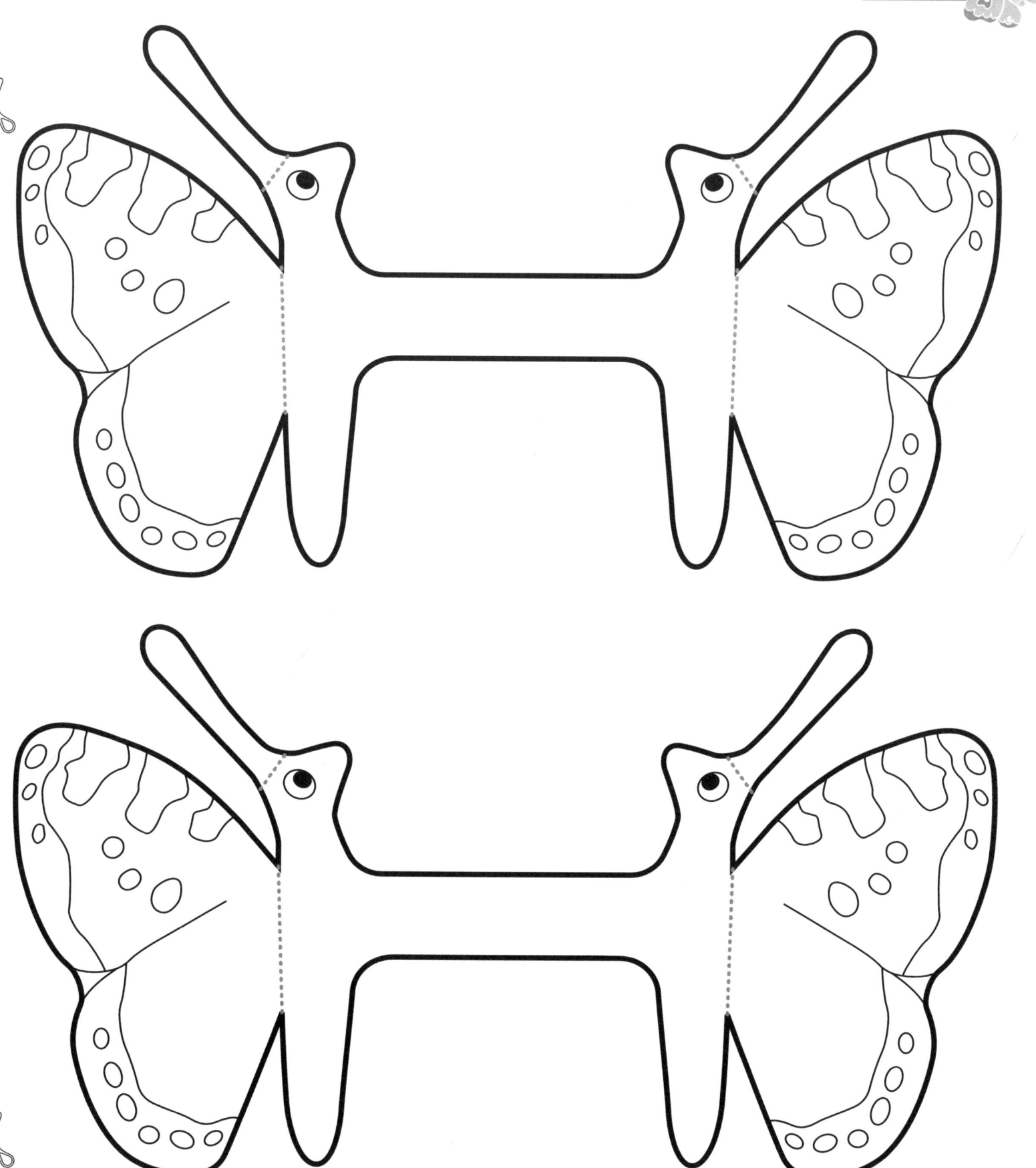

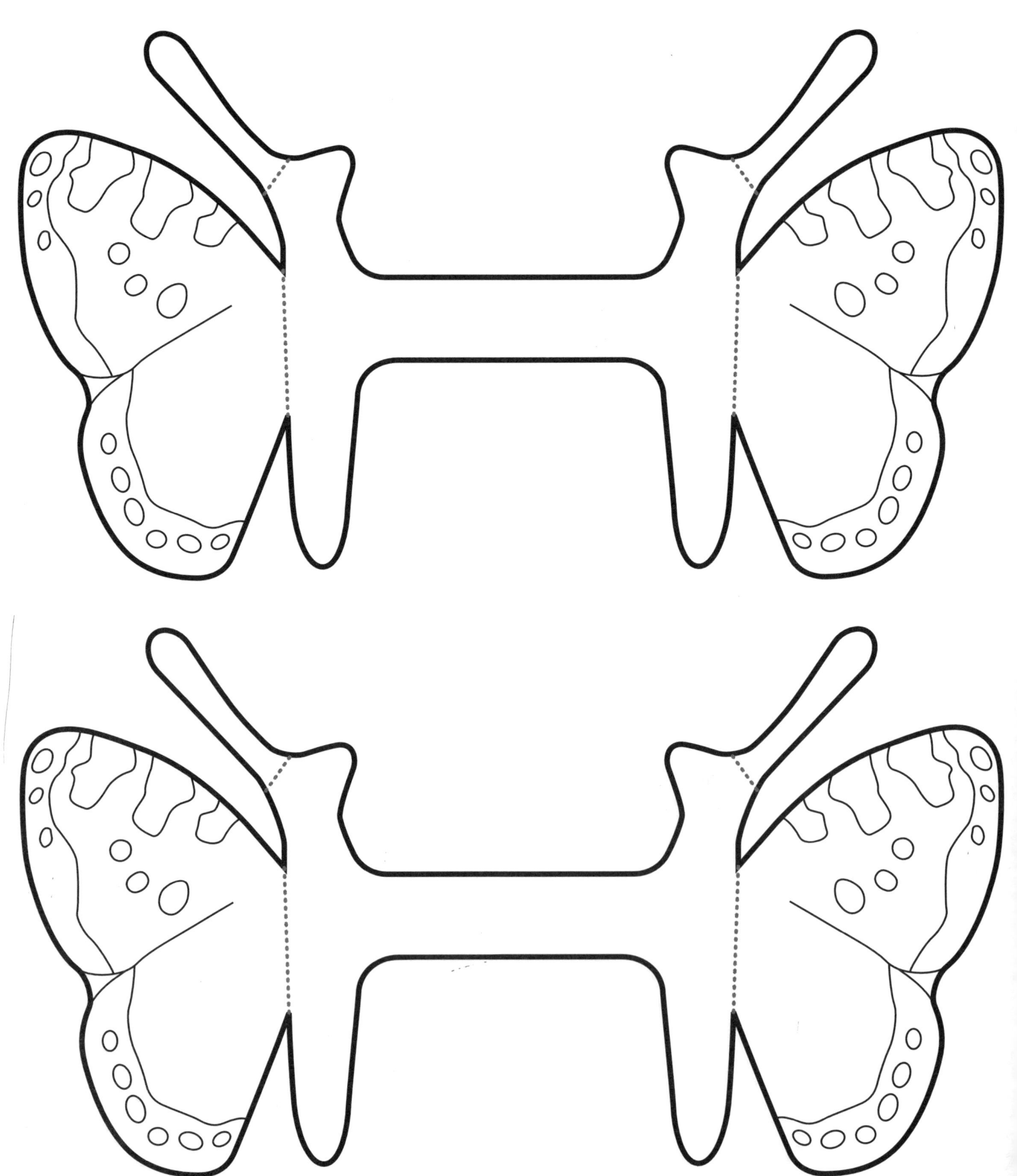

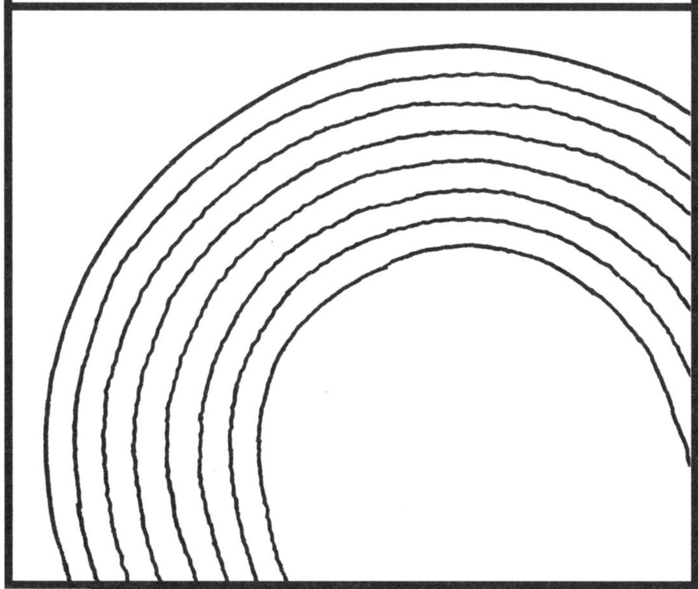

Cut Outs Story cards

Cut Outs Money

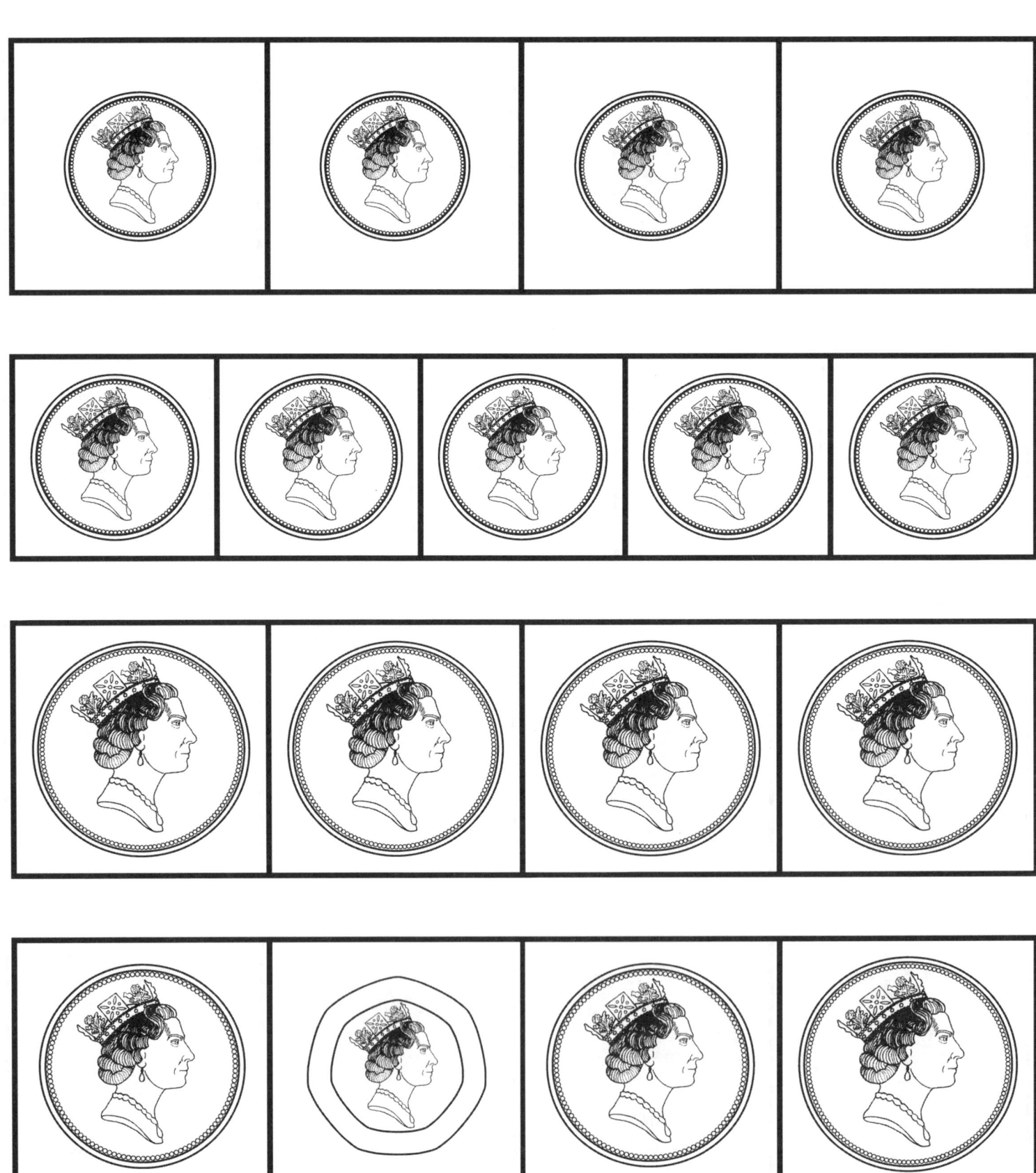

Cut Outs Face puzzles

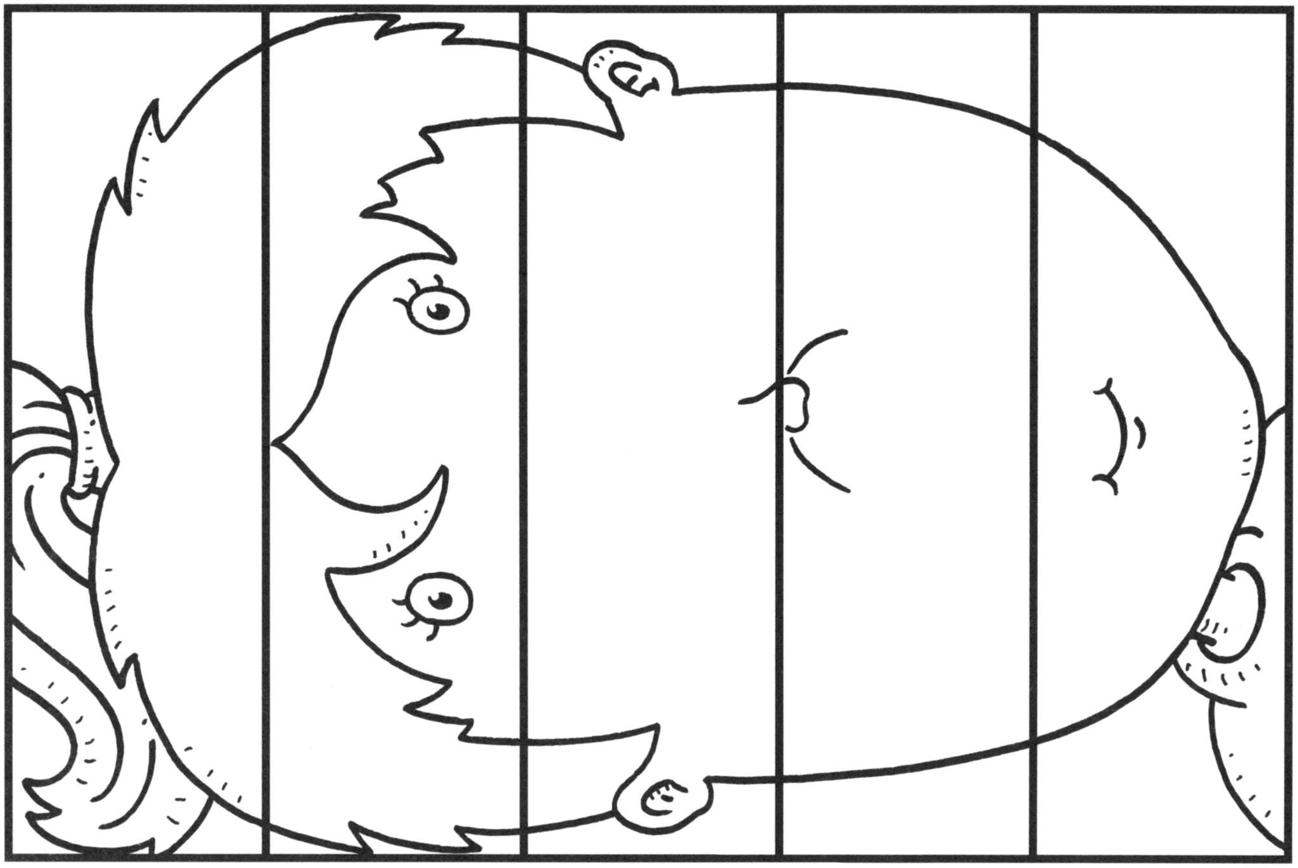

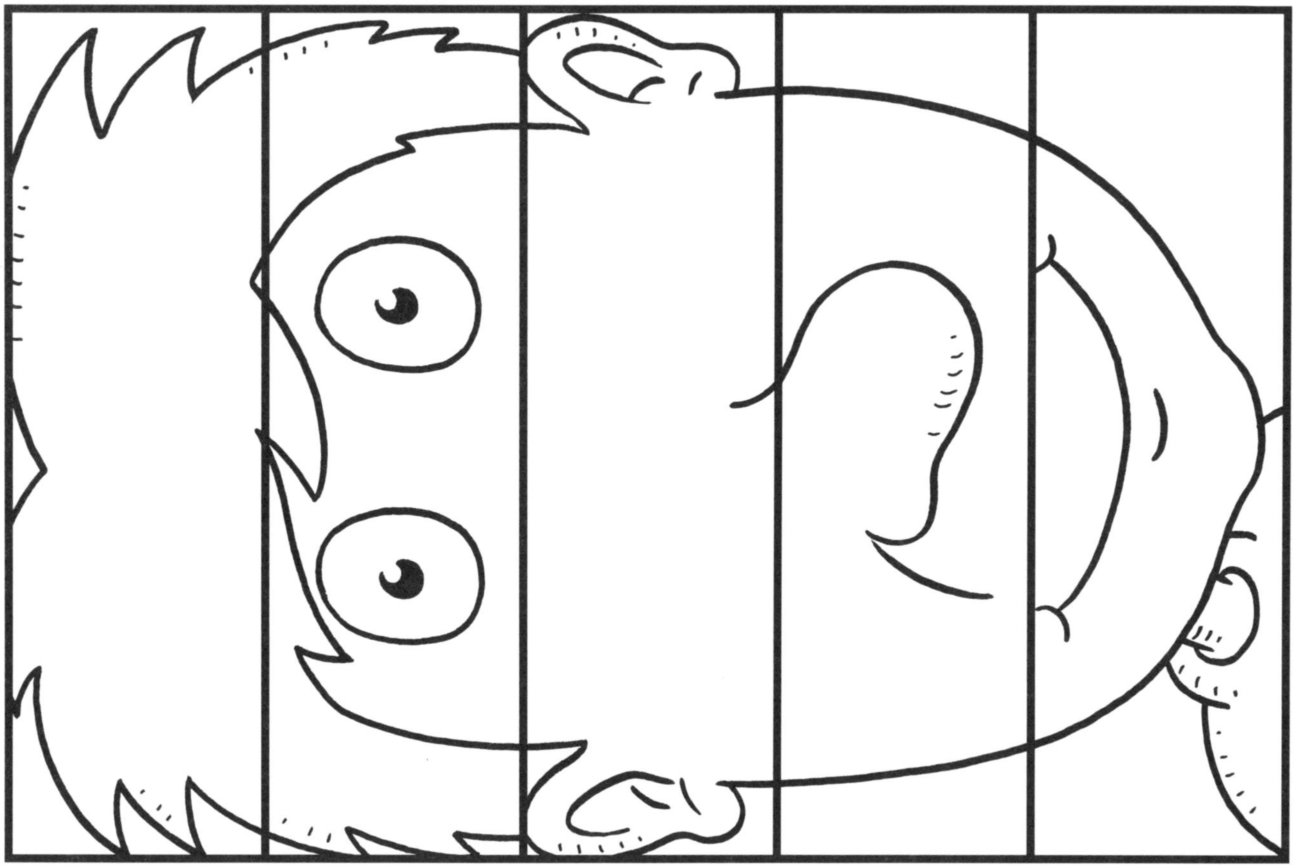

Cut Outs

Counters

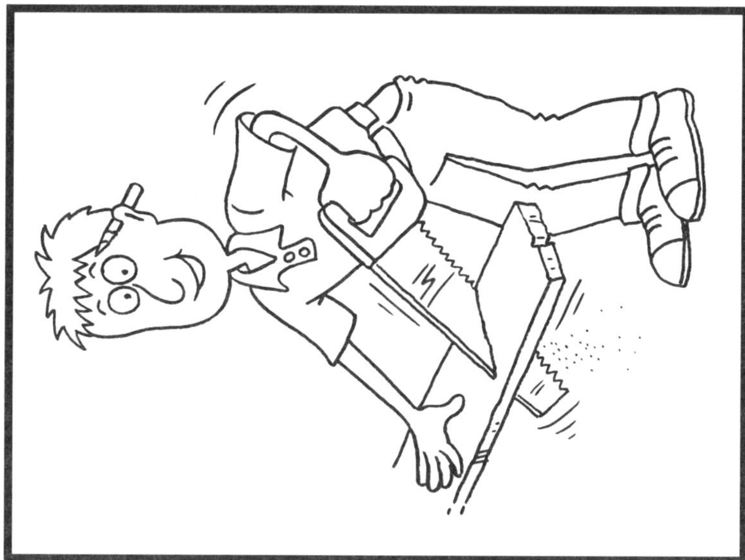

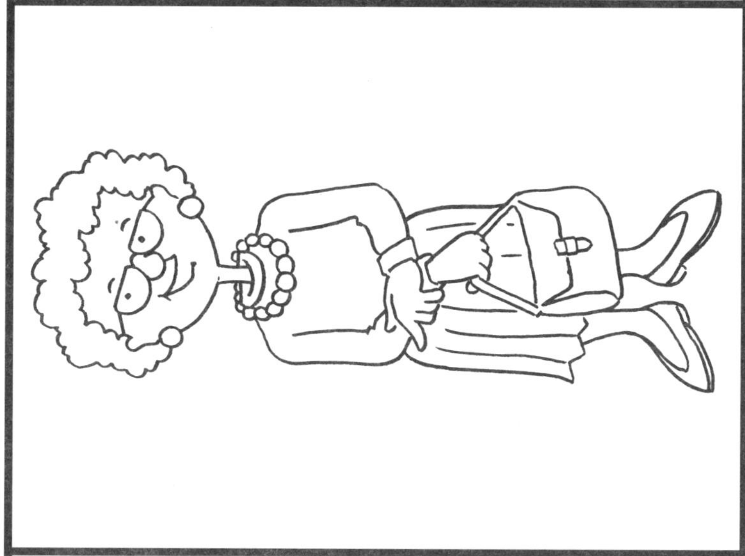

Cut Outs

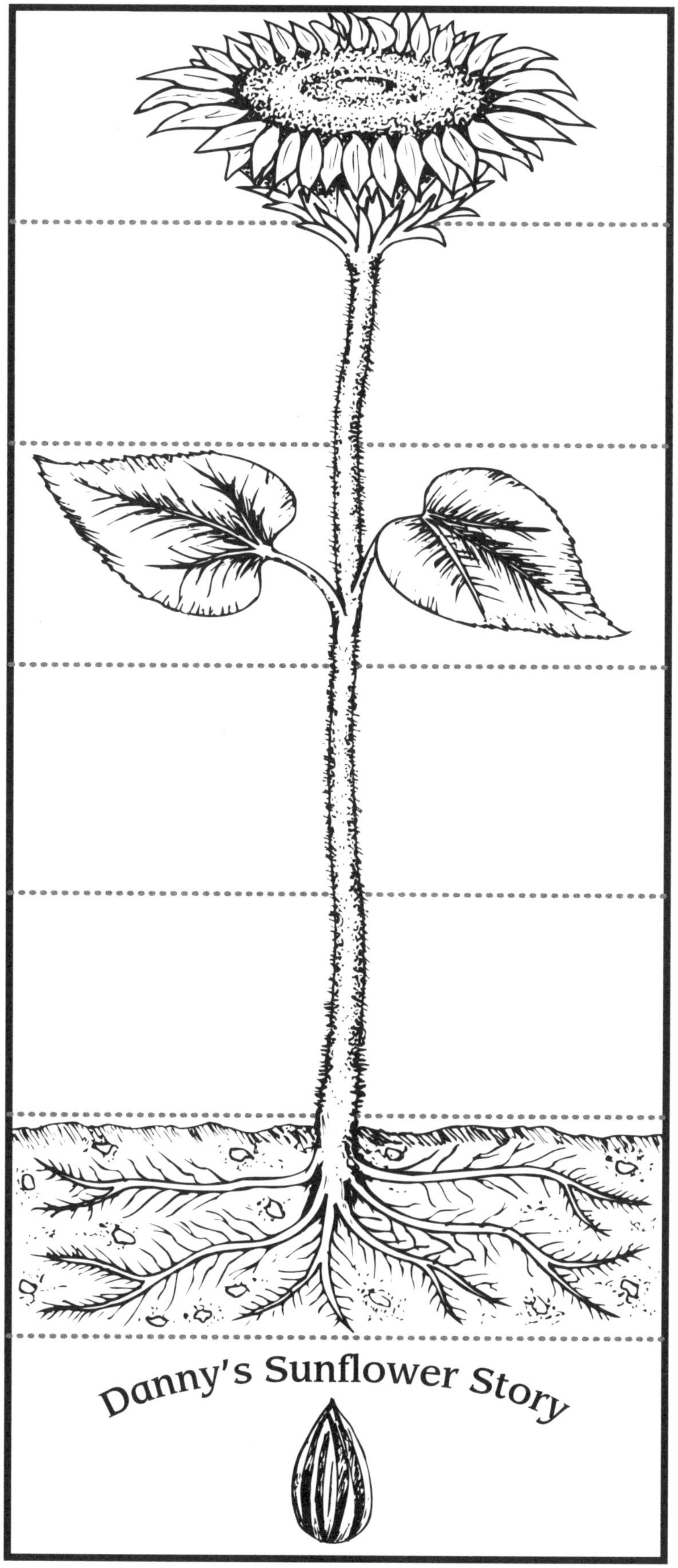

6

Sandwich

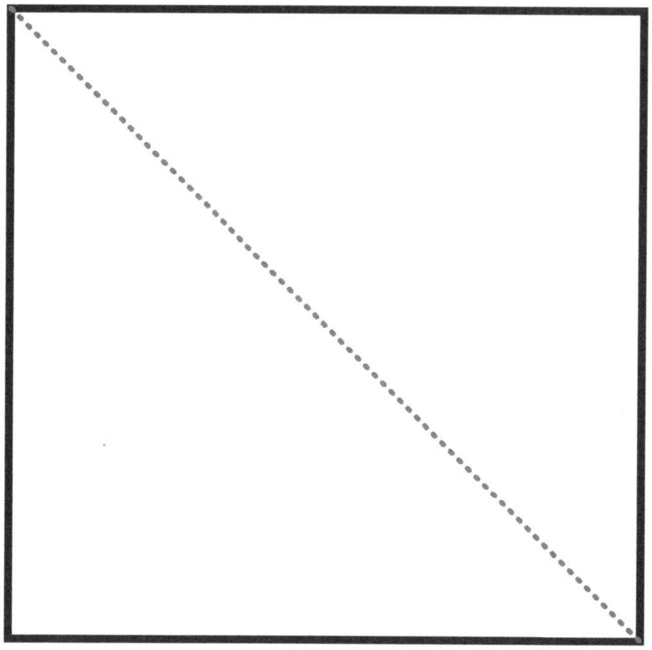

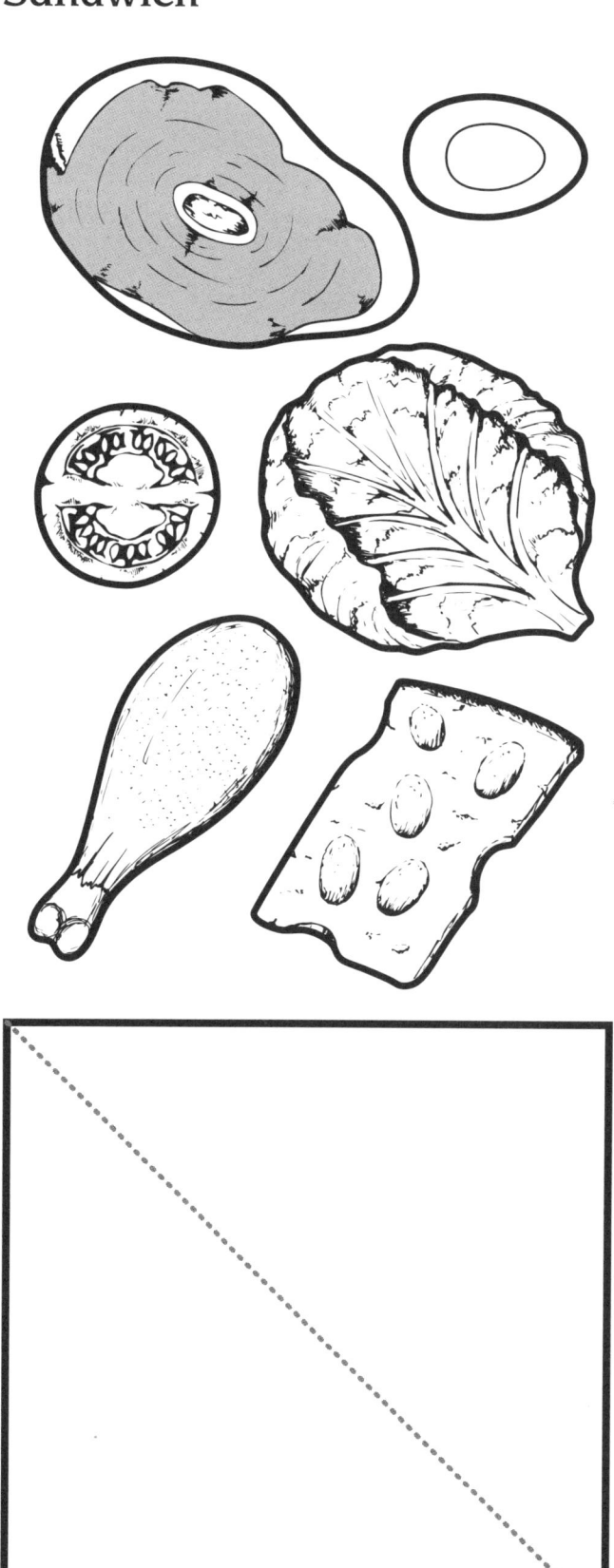

Danny's Sunflower Story

The sleeping cloud

Story characters

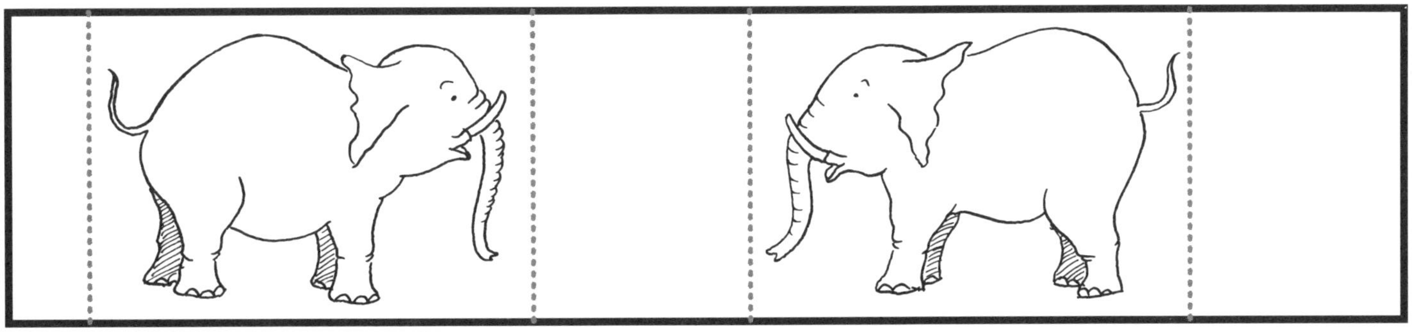

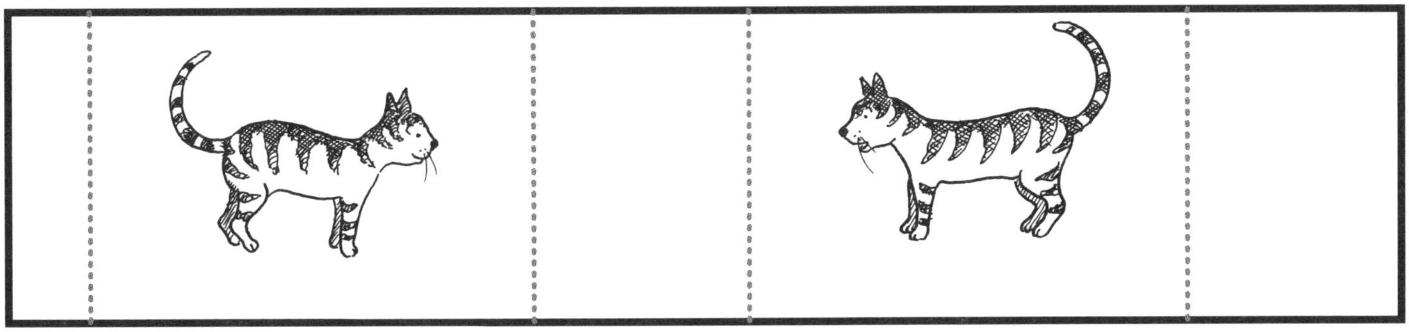

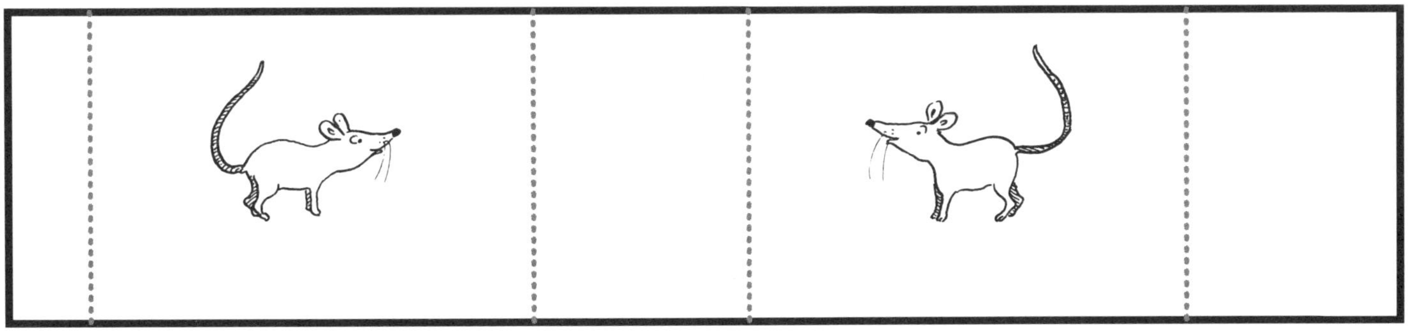

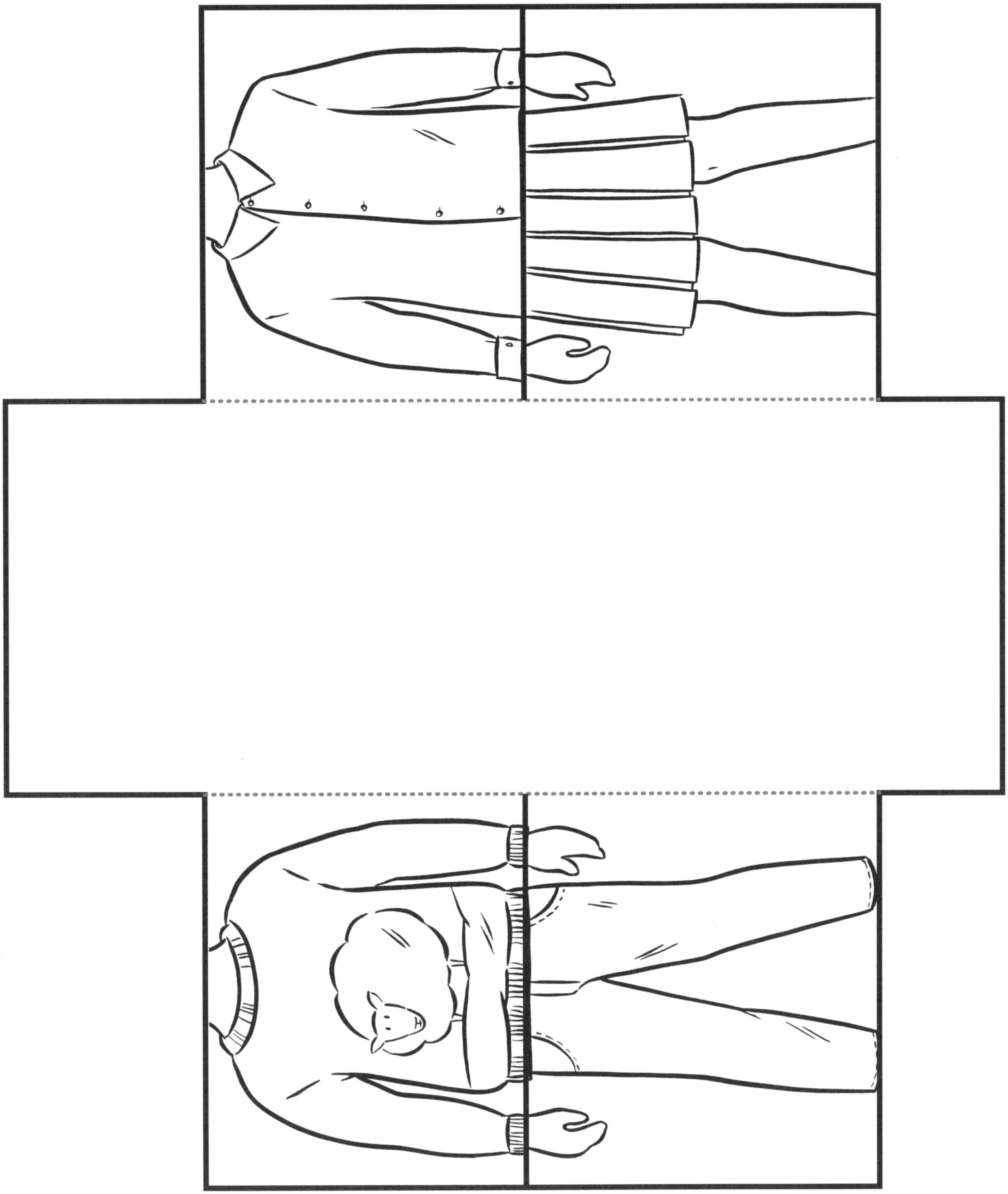

Cut Outs Clothes trick

7

Cut Outs Paper animals

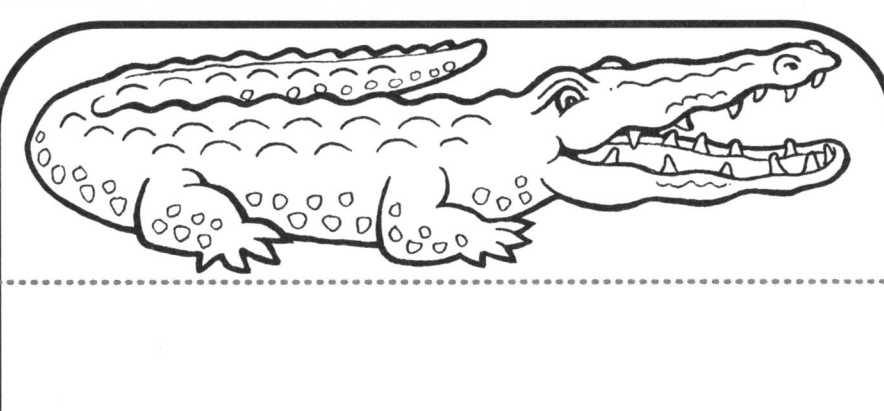

8

Cut Outs

Treasure hunt cards

Sing a song!	Count from 1 to 10.	Describe yourself.	Ask your friend a question.	Where do zebras and lions live?
Name three things in your classroom.	Talk about your favourite clothes.	Talk about your family.	Name three things in your pencil case.	Describe a friend.
Name three animals with six legs.	Say a poem or chant!	Name two foods you don't like.	Touch and name six parts of the body.	Name three rainforest animals.
Touch and name six colours.	Name four foods you like.	Count from 11 to 20.	Say what you're wearing today.	What's blue and yellow?

Treasure card	Treasure card	Treasure card	Treasure card	Treasure card
Treasure card	Treasure card	Treasure card	Treasure card	Treasure card
Treasure card	Treasure card	Treasure card	Treasure card	Treasure card
Treasure card	Treasure card	Treasure card	Treasure card	Treasure card

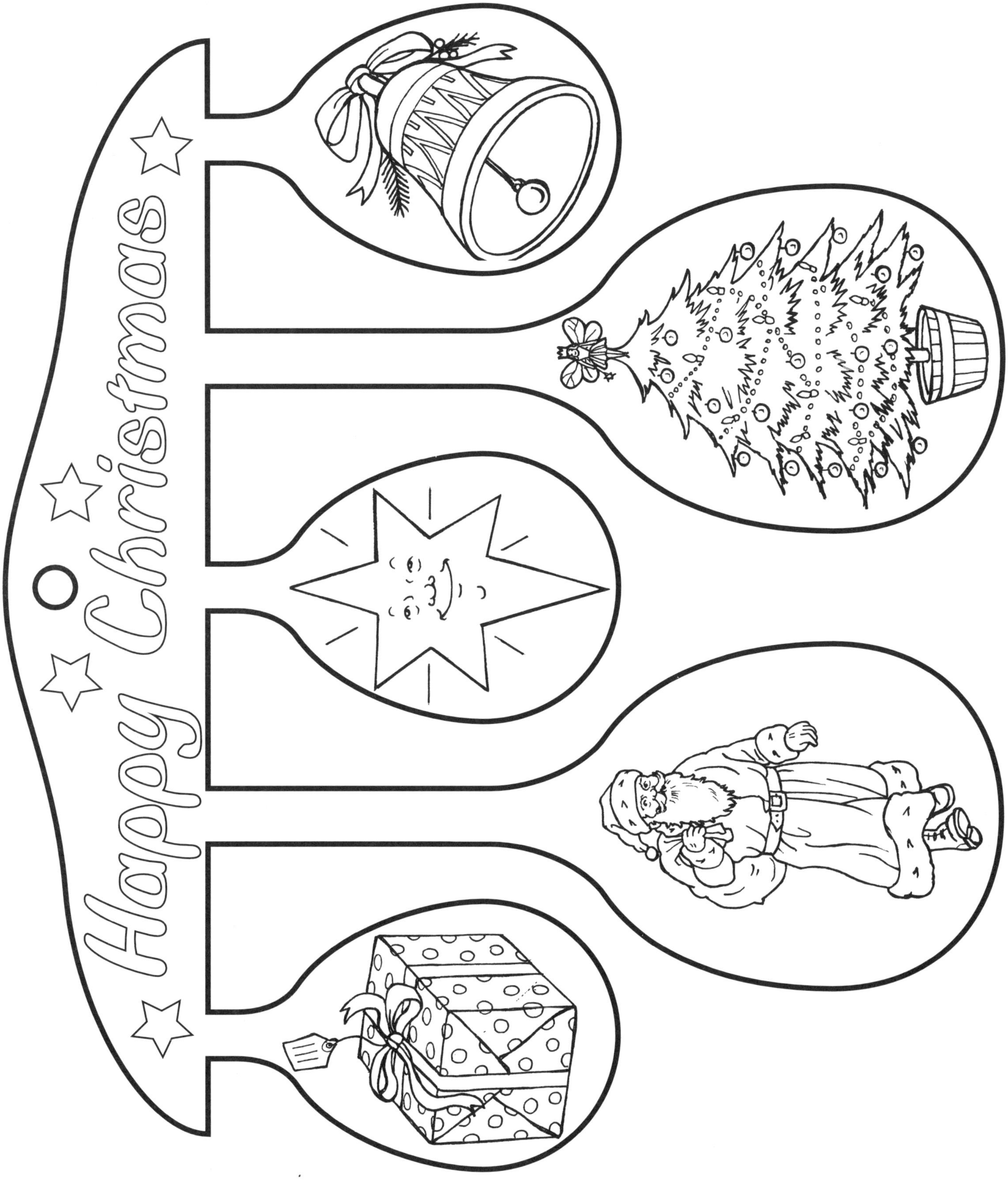

Cut Outs Christmas mobile

Happy Christmas

Cut Outs Easter card

HAPPY EASTER

Macmillan Education
Between Towns Road, Oxford OX4 3PP
A division of Macmillan Publishers Limited

Companies and representatives throughout the world.

ISBN 0 333 91634 4

First published 2000

Designed by Visual Image

Cover illustration by Roger Harris

Illustrated by: Lorna Kent, Amanda Abbit, Debi Ani,
John Bendall-Brunello, Kay Dixey, Hilary Evans, Michael Evans,
Kevin McAleenan, Karen Tushingham, Stella Voce.

Printed and bound in Spain by
Mateu Cromo S.A.

2004 2003 2002 2001
10 9 8 7 6 5 4 3 2